# Contents

## Introducing Paint Shop Pro 9 and Studio

1

## Selections

35

2

## Painting, drawing and text 59

**3**

# Introducing Paint Shop Pro 9 and Studio

In this chapter, you'll learn to use the Paint Shop Pro 9 and Studio screens and work with files. You'll also customize your working environment and create new toolbars. You'll rescale and resample images (and resize their canvas) then go on to learn about special screen modes. You'll also zoom in and out; use the Magnifier and Overview palette; and reverse/redo amendments. Finally, you'll learn how to work with background/foreground colors and swatches and how to use the Learning Center.

## Covers

**Chapter One**

# The Paint Shop Pro 9 screen

There are a lot of features in the Paint Shop Pro 9 screen but it is still easy to use.

*For the sake of convenience and brevity, this book will generally refer to "Paint Shop Pro 9" as "Paint Shop Pro" and "Paint Shop Pro Studio" as "Studio".*

Title bar     Menu bar     Toolbars     Materials palette

Tools toolbar     Rulers     Overview palette     Layers palette

*Your screen may look slightly different – in particular, you may have different or more palettes displaying. That's the fun of Paint Shop Pro: you can pretty much get your working environment looking the way you want it. See pages 14–16.*

Some of these features are unique to Paint Shop Pro.

## The Tools toolbar (or Tool palette)
You'll use this all the time to activate tools.

*For more on the Overview palette, see page 27.*

## The Materials palette
At first sight, palettes look quite different but they're actually toolbars. The Materials palette is something else you'll use very frequently, to access Paint Shop Pro's color selection tools.

# The Studio screen

Studio's opening screen has pretty much the same components as Paint Shop Pro's. However, it also has a useful, task-based Interactive Guide.

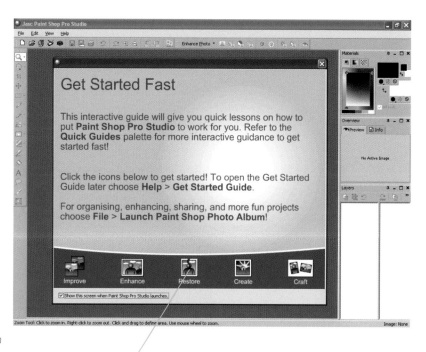

*Keep your version of Paint Shop Pro or Studio up to date. Select Help, Check for Updates and download the latest patches and fixes.*

Click an icon for a short introduction to associated Studio features

# Learning Center

Studio's Get Started Guide refers to topics in the Learning Center. This is a special palette that provides access to short, quick tutorials that provide essential tuition in core topics.

### Learning Center in Paint Shop Pro

1 Choose Help, Learning Center (or press F10)

2 Click a topic header

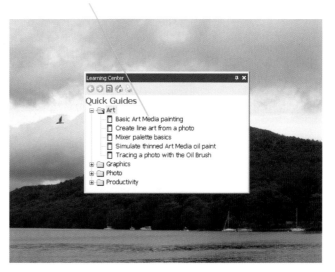

3 Work through the topic

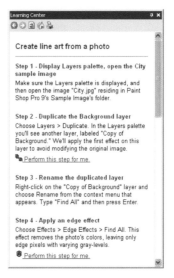

## Learning Center in Studio

1 Choose Help, Learning Center (or press F10)

2 Drill down to the topic you need then click it

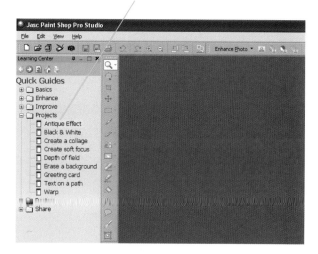

3 Work through the topic

# Guides

You can create guides in Paint Shop Pro pictures. Guides are useful alignment devices because you can ensure that selections, vector objects and brush strokes are automatically aligned with guides when they come within a specific distance.

### Creating guides

1 Ensure rulers are currently displayed (View, Rulers)

2 Click in the vertical or horizontal ruler and drag out a guide

3 To move a guide, drag the handle in the ruler to a new location

4 To specify the distance at which objects snap to guides, double-click a ruler. In the dialog, select the Guides tab. Type in a distance (in pixels) in the Snap influence field – the default is 15

## Recoloring guides

By default, guides are blue – this isn't always suitable since it often clashes with images. To apply a new color:

1 Double-click a guide's handle

2 Click here

3 Refer to the Color ring at the top of the Color dialog. Drag on the outer ring to select a hue,

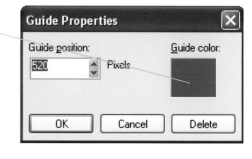

**Guide Properties**

Guide position:
520    Pixels

Guide color:

OK    Cancel    Delete

then drag in the inner square to adjust the saturation. When the Current color box shows the correct color, click OK

4 Click OK

## Applying grids

1 Grids are a lattice of horizontal/ vertical lines that you can use to align objects more accurately. To view (or hide) the grid, press Ctrl+Alt+G

2 To refine it (e.g. change the color), double-click a ruler and complete the dialog that appears

*If an image has both guides and a grid active, the grid is ignored.*

*To delete a guide, drag it by its handle till it's off the image window.*

*To have selections/vector objects align with guides, the Snap To Guides feature must be turned on. If it isn't, pull down the View menu and click Snap To Guides.*

# Customizing screen components

### Preliminaries

1. It's a good idea to calibrate your monitor before using Paint Shop Pro or Studio to any extent – calibration improves image quality

2. Go to www.jasc.com/support/kb/articles/monitor.asp

3. Follow the instructions

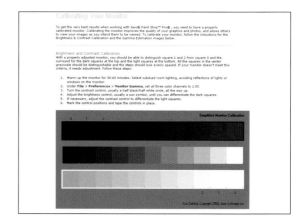

### Viewing/hiding components

1. In the View menu, click Grid, Guides or Rulers to enable or disable them

2. To show or hide toolbars, click Toolbars

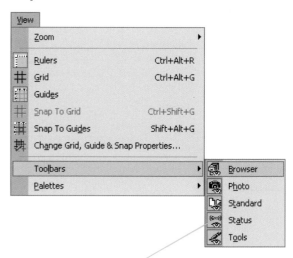

3. Click a toolbar entry to display or hide it – if it's lit, it's visible

# Menus/toolbars Paint Shop Pro 9 only

Paint Shop Pro 9 is almost infinitely customizable. You can:

- add program commands to toolbars, menus or palettes

- create your own toolbars

- allocate keyboard shortcuts to menu commands

## Adding or moving commands

1 Choose View, Customize

3 Drag the command to a toolbar, menu or palette

*To remove a menu, toolbar or palette command, follow step 1. Then drag the command into the work area and release the mouse button.*

2 Select a category on the left then a command on the right

4 To move an existing command, just drag its icon to a new menu, toolbar or palette

5 Hit Close in the dialog to confirm your changes

## Creating toolbars

Want your own toolbar? No problem.

1 Choose View, Customize

2 Select the Toolbars tab

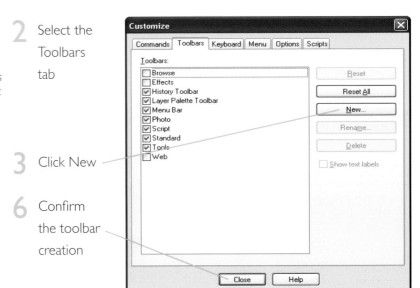

3 Click New

6 Confirm the toolbar creation

4 Name the toolbar and click OK

5 To populate the new toolbar, select the Commands tab in the Customize dialog then drag the relevant commands onto it (see page 15)

# Keyboard shortcuts Paint Shop Pro 9 only

*You can also assign icons to scripts – you can then drag the icons onto toolbars or menus. Click the Scripts tab then select a script/ icon combination. Click Bind.*

Being able to launch a command via a keyboard shortcut can save a lot of time and effort.

1 Choose View, Customize

2 Select the Keyboard tab

3 Select a category then a command

*Click in Set Accelerator for and choose whether you want the shortcut to work in the program itself (Default) or the Browser.*

4 Press the relevant keys then hit Assign

5 Confirm

## Viewing all shortcuts

1 For an overview of all Paint Shop Pro shortcuts, choose Help, Keyboard Map (you can also use this technique to view existing shortcuts in Studio)

*To print the shortcut list, click the Print icon.*

2 Shortcuts display by category/ command

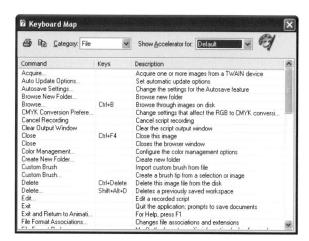

# Palettes

Paint Shop Pro organizes many of its key commands in "palettes". Palettes work just like toolbars. By default, they're positioned ("docked") on the right of the screen but they can also be dragged out like toolbars.

### Hiding/showing palettes

Choose View, Palettes. In the submenu, click any palette entry to display or hide it

### Making palettes float

Click any palette's Title bar and drag it onto your work area

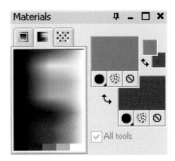

*You can resize the palette, too, just like any window.*

2 The "floating" palette – double-click the Title bar to redock it

### Using the Pushpin

Click the Pushpin symbol (if it's vertical, as here) to ensure that, when you move the cursor away from the palette, it remains fully displayed onscreen

*The Pushpin works when palettes are docked, too.*

2 If the Pushpin points to the left, click it to have the palette roll-up when not being used, so only its Title bar is visible:

# Opening files

Paint Shop Pro and Studio will open (i.e. read and display) numerous raster and bitmap graphics formats. When you tell either program to open an image, it recognizes its format by taking account of the file suffix – for example, TIFF (Tagged Image File Format) images must end in .TIF (they always do). Not all of the supported formats, however, can be written to disk.

## Opening images – the dialog route

1 Press Ctrl+O

2 Use the standard Open dialog that launches to find and open one or more images

## Opening images – the Browser route

1 Press Ctrl+B

2 Use the tree hierarchy to navigate to the folder that holds the image(s) you want to open

3 Double-click an image thumbnail

4 You can also carry out file house-keeping – for instance, copying/moving, renaming or deleting pictures. Right-click any thumbnail, select a command and complete any dialog that launches

# New files

*To duplicate the active image, click its Title bar (if you can't see it, hit Ctrl+W). Press Shift+D; Paint Shop Pro opens the copy in a new window.*

Often, images will be "ready-made" for you in the form of clip art or scanned pictures. However, there will be times when you'll need to create an image from scratch. There are several stages, but Paint Shop Pro makes this easy.

## Creating a new image

1 Press Ctrl+N

2 Select a preset e.g. "4 × 6 in horizontal"

3 If none of the presets are suitable, enter your own dimensions and resolution

*Resolution is defined as the measurement (usually expressed in dpi – dots per inch) of image sharpness. For Web pictures, use a resolution of 72 pixels per inch. With other pictures, a useful standard is 96–150 pixels per inch.*

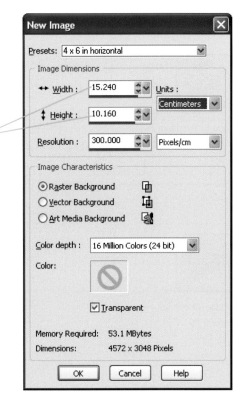

4 Select a background type, according to the type of image you want to work with. Don't forget your choice isn't cast in stone: you can always create a different layer type later and work on that

*See pages 167–168 for more on creating images with Art Media backgrounds.*

5 Set the color depth – remember that many filters, deformations and effects require a minimum of 16 million colors

6 Confirm the operation

# Importing

### Importing from TWAIN-compliant scanners/cameras

1 With your scanner/camera connected to your PC and the relevant software installed, choose File, Import, TWAIN, Select Source and select your device in the dialog

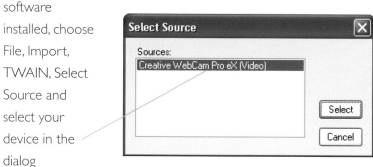

2 Choose File, Import, TWAIN, Acquire

3 Follow the onscreen instructions then refine the image in Paint Shop Pro or Studio

### Importing photos from WIA-compliant PCs

1 Select File, Import, From Scanner or Camera

### Importing photos from cameras that display as drives

1 These cameras display in Windows Explorer as mounted drives. Copy your photographs to your hard drive in the usual way

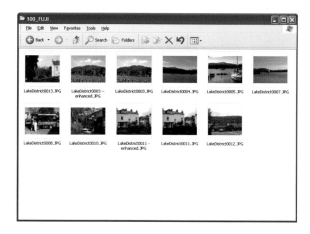

# Saving files

When you're working on one or more images in Paint Shop Pro, it's important to save your work at frequent intervals, in order to avoid data loss in the event of a hardware fault or power interruption.

*Re step 1 – Paint Shop Pro has its own proprietary format (suffix: .pspimage) that retains layers, vectors, masks and selection data. Use the Paint Shop Pro format while you're working with an image; when it's complete, save it to a nonproprietary format.*

### Saving an image for the first time

1  Select File, Save or press Ctrl+S

2  Paint Shop Pro or Studio launches a standard Save dialog. Use this to select an output format then save your image to disk

### Saving an image subsequently

1  Select File, Save or press Ctrl+S – this time, no dialog launches

### Saving a copy of an image

1  Select File, Save As or press F12. Complete the dialog but this time allocate a new name

### Autosave Paint Shop Pro 9 only

1  You can have Paint Shop Pro save your images automatically. In the event of a crash, it will automatically open autosaved images

2  Choose File, Preferences, Autosave settings

3  Enable Autosave then select a save interval

# Resizing/resampling

You can resize an image in various ways. This is useful for a variety of reasons, but especially if digital photos you've taken aren't the right size for printing.

## Resizing an image

1 Pull down the Image menu and click Resize (or hit Shift+S)

2 Select Percent or Pixels. Then amend the Width or Height fields

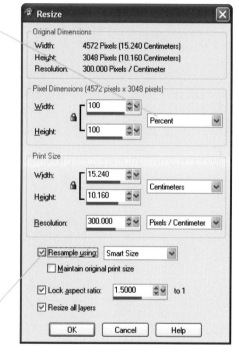

3 To change the size of the printed image, ensure Resample using in unchecked then specify new Width/ Height values or enter a new resolution

4 With Steps 2 and 3, the number of pixels remains unaltered. Check Resample using and select a resample type (variable according to the image type) if you want Paint Shop Pro or Studio to add new pixels in the course of resizing. Take care with this technique, however: it can degrade image quality. As a guide, don't enlarge a picture more than once and don't do so by more than 25%

5 Confirm the operation

# Enlarging the canvas

When you create a blank image, you specify the width and height in pixels. When you do this, Paint Shop Pro and Studio automatically define a "canvas" (the area on which the image lies) with the same dimensions. However, you can easily enlarge the canvas (e.g. if you need to resize the image).

*Enlarging an image's canvas (unlike resizing) does not expand the image itself.*

### Increasing an image's canvas

1 Select Image, Canvas Size

2 Choose a unit then insert increased Width and/or Height values (check Lock aspect ratio to resize the canvas proportionately)

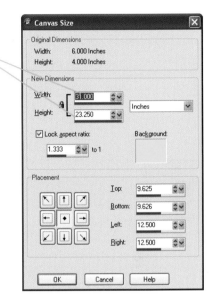

3 Select a background color

4 Optionally, enter new placement dimensions then click OK

5 Here, the canvas has been enlarged vertically and horizontally with the background set to yellow

# Zoom

Zooming in (magnifying) and zooming out (reducing magnification) are important when you're working with images.

## Zooming in and out in single increments

1 Click here in the Tool palette then click Zoom (or just press Z)

2 Position the mouse pointer where you want to zoom in/out then left-click to zoom in or right-click to zoom out

## More zoom precision

Make sure the Zoom tool is active then drag out a box – the area inside the box is magnified

## Using the Magnifier

1 Press Ctrl+Alt+M

2 Place the cursor on the area you want magnified – the Magnifier enlarges by the largest percentage possible, so the quality won't be high

*Many features in Paint Shop Pro and Studio are supplied with extremely useful features called "presets". Presets are essentially scripts that define the way tools and dialogs operate. We'll look at scripts in more detail in Chapter 9 but in the meantime it's useful to examine how zoom presets work. There are no supplied zoom presets but you can easily create your own.*

## Zoom presets

1 Press Z to activate the Zoom tool

2 If the Tool Options palette isn't onscreen, press F4

3 Click here. Select the Save (disk) icon in the new dialog then create a preset

4 Alternatively, enter a zoom percentage (1–5000) into the Zoom (%) box in the palette

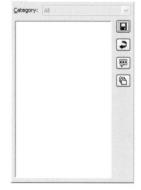

# Overview palette

When you've zoomed in on part of an image, Paint Shop Pro lets you view the entire image at the same time (in a way, this is the opposite of using the Magnifier). You do this by launching the Overview palette.

### Using the Overview palette

1 If the Overview palette isn't visible, either on the right of the screen (the default) or as a toolbar, press F9

2 If an image is being viewed at a high magnification and not all of it displays in its window, the Overview palette shows a rectangle representing the visible area. Drag this to view a new area in the main window

3 Select the Info tab for brief information about the picture

# Special screen modes Paint Shop Pro 9 only

There are two special screen modes that show more of the open picture and fewer extraneous screen components.

*Any attempt to edit your image in Full Screen Preview will revert to the normal editing mode.*

1 Hit Ctrl+Shift+A to enter Full Screen Preview mode (Esc to return to the normal screen):

2 Press Shift+A to enter Full Screen Edit mode (repeat this to close):

*Full Screen Edit hides the Title, Menu and Status bars. Use this when you want to work with your picture.*

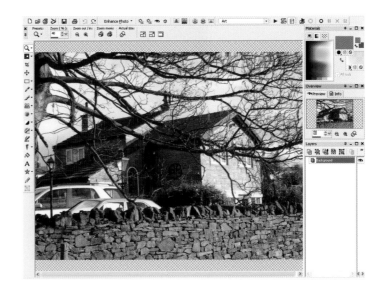

# Tabbing images

If you regularly work with several images open at once, you'll probably find this technique extremely useful. Instead of the images displaying as separate windows, you can have them tabbed across the top of the screen.

1 With several images open, select Window, Tabbed Documents

2 Tabs representing each image appear at the top of the screen – the image currently displayed is in bold

3 It's now impossible to minimize or maximize image windows

4 To view a different image, click its tab

5 To view images normally again, select Window, Tabbed Documents

# History palette Paint Shop Pro 9 only

The History palette lists every command you apply to an image. You can then select a series of consecutive commands and undo them. Even better, you can selectively undo an action and leave subsequent ones intact.

*You can also undo the latest action by pressing Ctrl+Z. Ctrl+Alt+Z*

*redoes it*

1 If the History palette isn't onscreen, press F3

2 This image has been amended in four ways: see below for details. The commands are listed sequentially in the History

*Undoing single commands while leaving untouched later ones can sometimes yield unpredictable results.*

palette, with the most recent at the top and the earliest at the bottom of the palette

*You can save one or more commands as a special script. Just click the Save Quickscript button on the right of the palette.*

3 To undo a series of actions, select the latest one then click here

4 To redo a series of actions, select the latest one then click here

5 To undo one action (ignoring later ones), click here

6 To redo any single action undone in Step 5, click here

# Reverting

Another technique you can use to undo editing actions is reverting. When you revert an image, you discard all editing operations and return to the last saved version. The advantage reverting has over undoing actions is that it's comprehensive and almost instantaneous. In fact, it's the equivalent of closing the image, declining to save your amendments and then reopening it – Paint Shop Pro and Studio do most of the work for you.

1 This image has had an effect applied to it and various other changes

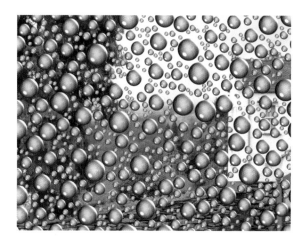

2 Select File, Revert to return to the status quo then click Yes in the message box

3 The original image, after all the edits have been removed

# Background/foreground colors

Paint Shop Pro and Studio use two broad color definitions – these are called "active" colors. Both are crucial to the way you work.

### Foreground colors

These occupy image foregrounds and are applied with the left mouse button.

### Background colors

These occupy backgrounds – apply them with the right button.

You apply both colors via the Materials palette.

### The Materials palette

*If you're working with images with fewer than 16 million colors, only 256 colors display in the Select Color panel. This means that when you select a color, that color which is nearest to the one selected is used, so it may not be what you want. For this reason, you may find it useful to have the Select Color panel only display the available 256 colors. Select File, Preferences, General Program Preferences. In the dialog, select the Palettes tab. Activate Show document palette. Click OK.*

1  If the Materials palette isn't visible (by default, on the right of the screen), press F6

2  These boxes are the Foreground and Background colors

3  The 3 tabs are (from left to right) Frame, Rainbow and Swatches

4  The Select Color panel – see the facing page

5  The two sizable boxes on the right are the Foreground/Stroke and Background/Fill boxes

## Selecting a color via the Frame tab

1  Select the Frame tab

*The reason for the existence of Foreground Stroke and Background Fill boxes as well as Foreground and Background color boxes is that the former also display gradients and patterns. Even when gradients and patterns are displaying, you can use the Foreground and Background color boxes to apply new colors without having to change the gradients or patterns.*

2  Left-click the outer rectangle to select the foreground color or right-click it to set the background color

3  Drag the horizontal slider to set the color's saturation

*If you don't want to apply a gradient or pattern, click the Transparent icon in the Foreground or Background Material boxes.*

4  Drag the vertical slider to set the color's lightness

## Selecting a color via the Rainbow tab

1  Select the Rainbow tab

2  Move the mouse pointer over the Select Color panel – it changes to an eyedropper

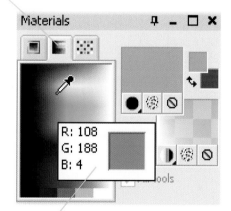

*As a general rule, use the left mouse button to apply foreground effects and the right to apply background effects. (This does not apply to a few tools e.g. the Text tool.)*

3  Left-click to select the foreground color or right-click to set the background color

4  A ToolTip shows the selected color value

# Swatches

## Selecting a swatch

1. Select the Swatches tab

2. Left-click the new swatch to select it as the foreground material or right-click to select it as the background material

*You can also work the process in the opposite way. Create a color/material in the Material dialog then click the Add to swatches button. Name the swatch and hit OK.*

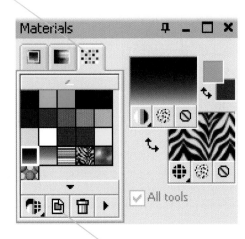

## Creating a swatch

1. To save color/material combinations for later reuse, click here

2. Name the swatch and click OK

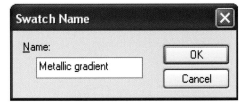

*Swatches are great timesavers. They're materials (i.e. colors or combinations of colors and gradients, patterns etc.) that you save for later reuse.*

## Editing a swatch

1. Double-click the swatch in the Materials palette

2. Edit the swatche's style or texture

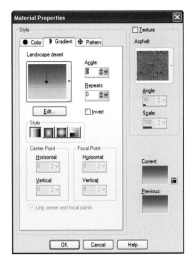

# Selections

In this chapter, you'll define a wide variety of bitmap selections (even exotic ones like stars). You'll deselect, invert and move selections then amend feathering. You'll also select image areas by more advanced methods based on color and then manipulate them. You'll save selections to disk and as alpha channels then create multiple/subtractive selections. Finally, you'll select and group vectors.

## Covers

Chapter Two

# Selections

*Don't run away with the idea that Studio is an inferior product to Paint Shop Pro 9. It's slightly less advanced, certainly, and has a somewhat different emphasis but it has lots of features that aren't beginner-level. For example, it will let you create all of the selection types listed on the right.*

Selecting all or part of a Paint Shop Pro image is the essential preliminary for performing any of its many editing operations.

You can make the following kinds of selections:

- rectangular, square, elliptical and circular

- triangular or hexagonal/octagonal/polygonal

- star- or arrow-shaped

- freehand

- color-based

- additive and subtractive

*Briefly, bitmaps consist of pixels (colored dots) while vectors are based on mathematical formulas. Care must be taken when resizing bitmaps that image quality isn't degraded.*

Additionally, you can select an entire image (including vectors) in one go – just press Ctrl+A.

You can also save image selections to disk as special files (and then reopen them at will within other images) and group/ungroup vector selections.

*The selection types listed above are bitmap (raster) selections. However, you can also select vector objects you've created earlier.*

A typical rectangular selection in Paint Shop Pro 9

# Selection borders

*You can convert ("promote") raster and vector selections into raster layers (but note that the part of the new layer not containing the selection is transparent). Simply pull down the Selections menu and press Ctrl+Shift+P.*

Generally, whenever you make a bitmap selection in Paint Shop Pro, you'll select part of an image. Whether you do this or select an image in its entirety, the portion you've selected is surrounded with a dotted line:

*There are occasions when it's useful to hide raster selection marquees – for instance, when you've applied feathering and want to see the result more clearly. Note that hiding marquees does not cancel the selection; it's still there. (To hide the active selection's marquee, pull down the Selections menu and click Hide Marquee. Or press Ctrl+Shift+M.)*

A freehand selection in Studio

As with most programs, the selection border (sometimes called a "marquee" or "marching ants") moves and so is easy to locate.

## Differences

Paint Shop Pro 9 and Studio handle selections in very similar ways. In the course of this chapter, we'll highlight any differences as we encounter them.

# Selection modes

You can use two kinds of bitmap selection:

## Standard

These form part of the original image. If you move a selection area, the resultant gap is filled with the background color.

## Floating

When a selection area is floating, the contents are on top of (and distinct from) the original.

## Floating v. Standard selections:

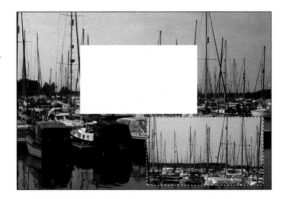

A Standard selection. The selection has been moved, filling the gap with the active background

A Floating selection. As above, but the underlying image is unaffected

To float a selection, press Ctrl+F. To defloat a selection (return it to Standard), press Ctrl+Shift+F

# Creating rectangular selections

You can create rectangular bitmap selections in two ways:

- with the use of the mouse

- with the use of a special dialog

### The mouse route

Ensure the Tool palette is onscreen (if it isn't, right-click any toolbar or palette – in the menu, select Toolbars, Tools). Then carry out the following steps:

*To specify the amount of feathering (the sharpness of the selection), type in a value in the Feather field. The range is from 0 (maximum sharpness) to 200 (maximum softness).*

Click here in the Tool palette then click Selection (or just press S)

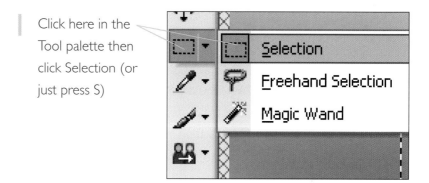

If the Tools toolbar isn't onscreen, right-click the Tool Palette and select Palettes, Tool Options (or just press F4)

*Less common is the need to create triangular, hexagonal, octagonal, polygonal, star- or arrow-shaped selections, but they can sometimes be useful and you can do this in both Paint Shop Pro 9 and Studio. Just select any of these in the drop-down list then drag it out.*

Click here and select Rectangle (or Rounded Rectangle to round off the corners) in the drop-down menu

*To create a square selection with the mouse, follow steps 1–2 on page 39. In step 3, select Square (or Rounded Square) instead.*

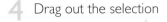 Drag out the selection

## The dialog route

Refer to the Tool Options palette and do the following:

*This is one of the many areas where Paint Shop Pro 9 and Studio use identical procedures.*

Click here

Type in the positions (in pixels) of the four corners (enter the same dimension four times to make a square) then click OK

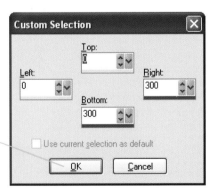

# Creating elliptical selections

1  Press S to launch the Selection Tool

2  If it isn't already onscreen, launch the Tools toolbar

3  In the Selection type field, select Ellipse

*To create a circular selection, just select Circle in step 3 then drag it out.*

4  Drag to define the selection

# Irregular selections

As we've seen, you can use the Freehand tool to create selections by hand. This needs a steady hand and ideally a certain amount of artistic ability.

## Creating freehand selections

Ensure the Tool Palette is onscreen (if it isn't, right-click any toolbar or palette and select Toolbars, Tools). Then:

1 Click here in the Tool palette then click Freehand Selection

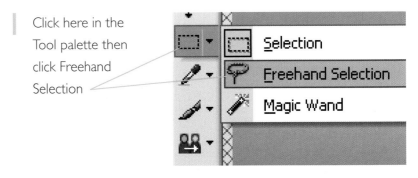

*You can refine freehand selections. To avoid the selection having irregular borders, click in the Selection type field and select Point to point (the borders are straight), Smart Edge (the borders are defined between contrasting colors/light) or Edge Seeker (Paint Shop Pro locates edges in areas with slight color/light changes).*

2 If you've saved any freehand presets earlier, click here and go to step 3

4 Complete any of the Tool Options toolbar settings. For example, type in a Feather setting (in the range: 0–200)

*Consider unchecking Anti-alias if you're not working with text or merging pictures (anti-aliasing works like feathering to smooth image edges, but is more precise).*

3 Select a preset

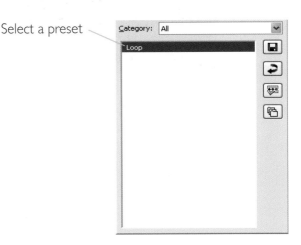

5 Drag to define the selection. Or, if you're using Point to point, Smart Edge or Edge Seeker, click around the area you want to select then double-click when you've finished

6 This is Edge Seeker in action — experiment with the Tools toolbar settings until you get the precision you need

# Selections based on color

You can use another Paint Shop Pro tool – the Magic Wand – to select portions of the active image which share a specific color.

### Creating color-based selections

Ensure the Tools toolbar is onscreen (if it isn't, right-click any toolbar or palette and select Toolbars, Tools). Then:

Click here in the Tools toolbar then click Magic Wand

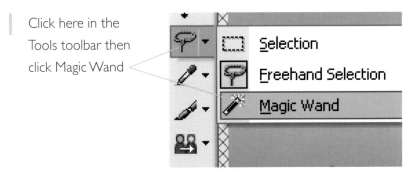

*Type in a value in the Tolerance field. (Tolerance is the degree to which image pixels must approach the chosen one to activate selection.) The permissible range is 0 (only exact matches result in selection) to 200 (all pixels are selected).*

2 If you've saved any freehand presets and want to use one now, click here and go to step 3

4 Complete any of the Tool Options toolbar settings. For example, type in a Feather setting (in the range: 0–200)

*Check Sample merged to make a selection based on all (not just the active) layers.*

3 Select a preset

5 Place the mouse pointer over the area you want to select and left-click once

*To remove a specific color from an existing selection, follow steps 1–4 on the facing page. Now hold down Ctrl as you click the color.*

6 The new selection

# Inverting raster selections

When you've selected a portion of a bitmap, you can have Paint Shop Pro deselect the selected area AND select the external area which was previously unselected, all in one operation. Paint Shop Pro calls this "inverting a selection".

Use inversion as a means of creating selections which would otherwise be difficult – or impossible – to achieve. Inversion is especially useful when you're working with photographs of people set against a single-color background. Select the background and then invert it as a really useful way to select the person. Much easier and quicker than using the Freehand tool.

### Inverting a selection

1 Make a normal selection then press Ctrl+Shift+I

2 A standard circular selection

In the "After" illustration, Paint Shop Pro has also surrounded the selected area with a dotted border.

3 After – the marquee now encloses the unselected area

# Moving raster selections

Paint Shop Pro lets you move bitmap selections (by detaching them from the host layer). You can move just the frame which defines the selection area or the frame together with the contents.

## Moving selection frames only

1 Ensure the selection you want to move isn't floating (if it is, press Ctrl+Shift+F)

*If you perform this technique on floating images (Ctrl+F) you'll move the frame AND contents.*

2 Press M to activate the Move tool

*To move just a marquee, you must use the Move tool. If you right-click in it with the original Selection tool, you'll deselect it instead. If you left-click and drag with the original tool, you'll move the selection content as well as the marquee.*

3 Right-click inside the selection area then drag it to a new location

...cont'd

*You can also move selections and their contents with the keyboard. Ensure the relevant selection tool is active. Hold down Shift. Now press and hold down any of the cursor keys. (Hold down Ctrl and Shift to increase the move speed.)*

## Moving bitmap selection frames and contents

First, ensure that the selection area is Standard or Floating, according to the effect you want to achieve. (See page 38 for a description of the two possible effects). Then:

1   In the Tool palette, activate the tool which was used to create the selection

2   Drag the selection to a new location

*The procedures in the above tip also apply to selected vector objects (except that the underlying image is unaffected).*

3   Moving the contents of a Standard selection (the original area is filled with the background color)

*Hold down Ctrl and Alt while pressing any of the arrow keys to simultaneously copy the selection (leaving the original unaffected) AND move it one pixel at a time.*

4   Moving the contents of a Floating selection

# Amending selection feathering

*If you've previously saved a feather preset, click in the Presets field and select it. Or click the Save icon to create a preset based on the step 2 setting.*

When you define a selection, you can feather it. You can also do this after the selection has been created.

## Imposing a new feathering

1 Define a selection then press Ctrl+H

*Feathering is useful: it helps a selection blend into the area around it. However, moving selections can leave some of the surrounding pixels attached to the selection border. Fortunately, Paint Shop Pro 9 (but not Studio) has an easy solution: matting. If the selection is on a black or white background, choose Selections, Matting, Remove Black Matte or Selections, Matting, Remove White Matte. If it's a colored background, however, select Matting, Defringe.*

2 Enter a feathering value in the range 0–200 (the preview on the right is updated)

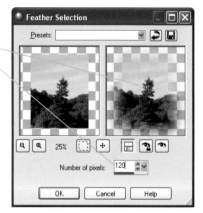

3 Magnified view of the feathered selection edge – this selection has been dragged to the right

*Matting also cleans up layers created from selections.*

# Selecting a color range

You can specify a color and tell Paint Shop Pro to add it to (or take it away from) a selection.

*You can create and use your own range presets in the Presets field.*

## Selecting a color

1 Define a selection then pull down the Selections menu and click Modify, Select Color Range

*Tolerance is the degree to which image pixels must approach the chosen one to activate selection. Use the range 0 (only exact matches result in selection) to 256 (all pixels are selected).*

2 Click the Reference color field. Select a color in the dialog or close it then (as here) click in the image to select the color you want to add or subtract

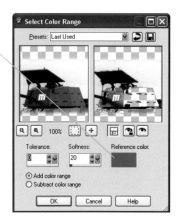

3 Select Add color range or Subtract color range then specify Tolerance and Smoothness settings. Click OK

*In this example, a rectangular selection was made around the turret, then one of the turret colors was selected (with a low tolerance) in step 2. When the frame was moved to the left, all colors apart from the selected one were moved.*

4 Moving this selection illustrates color range selection – see the DON'T FORGET tip

# Reusing selections

Paint Shop Pro lets you save a selection area (but not the contents) to disk as a special file. You can then load it into the same or a new image. This is a convenient way to reuse complex selections.

## Saving a selection

1 To save a selection to disk (with the extension: .PspSelection), choose Selections, Load/Save Selection, Save Selection to Disk

2 Name the selection then click Save

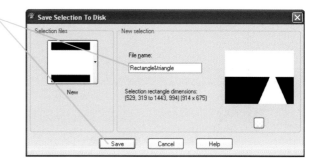

## Loading a selection

1 To reopen the selection into the same or a new image, choose Selections, Load/Save Selection, Load Selection From Disk

2 Select a selection, choose how it's added then click Load

# Selection additions/subtractions

*When you create multiple selections, a plus sign is added to the cursor for the relevant tool.*

You can define multiple (additive) selections. This is a very useful technique that enables you to create spectacular effects. You can also create selections subtractively, where Paint Shop Pro decreases the size of a selection in line with further contiguous selections you define.

## Creating multiple (additive) selections

Define the first selection, using any of the techniques previously discussed:

*If you define the second selection so that it does not touch the first, this creates two separate selections.*

Here, a rectangular selection has been created

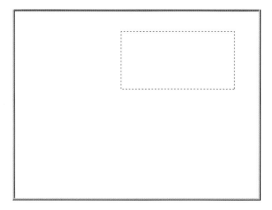

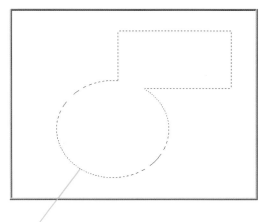

A further elliptical selection has been defined (forming one unusual selection)

*Re step 2 – if you're using the Magic Wand to create multiple selections, simply hold down Shift as you click the area you want to add.*

2 Hold down Shift, then define another selection

## Creating subtractive selections

1 Define the first selection, using any of the techniques previously discussed

*When you perform selection subtractions, Paint Shop Pro adds a minus sign to the cursor for the selection tool.*

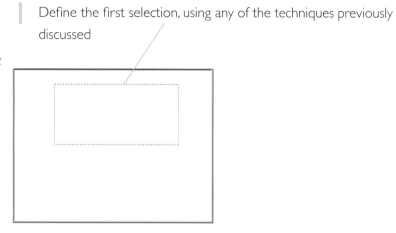

*If you're using the Magic Wand tool, simply hold down Ctrl as you click within the first selection area – Paint Shop Pro subtracts the second selection from the first.*

2 Hold down Ctrl as you define another contiguous selection then release the mouse button

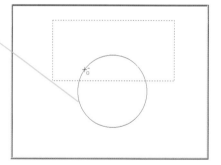

3 Paint Shop Pro has "subtracted" the second selection from the first

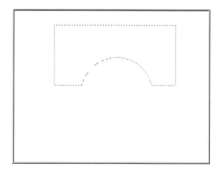

# Advanced selection operations

## Expanding/contracting selections by specific pixels

1 To contract or expand bitmap selections uniformly, choose Selections, Modify, Contract or Selections, Modify, Expand

*You can create and use your own range presets in the Presets field.*

2 In the Number of pixels: field, type in the extent of the contraction or expansion (in the range: 0–100 pixels). Finally, click OK

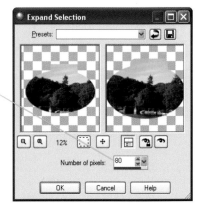

## Expanding selections by color values

1 To expand bitmap selections based on color values, choose Selections, Modify, Select Similar

2 Enter a Tolerance setting (in the range: 0–200)

*This can be an extremely useful technique. Here, selecting a small area in the house (the left screen) has resulted in nearly all of it being selected on the right (without the unwanted background). Customize the Tolerance value until you get exactly the result you want. Remember you can zoom in and out using the Zoom buttons under the left screen.*

3 Select Contiguous (for adjacent matches) or Discontiguous (for matches anywhere in the image) then click OK to confirm

## Imposing borders on selections

After you've defined a selection, you can border it. Once you've done this, you can then fill the border with the Flood Fill tool or apply an effect to it.

*It's sometimes useful to smooth out selection edges. Choose Selections, Modify, Smooth then experiment with the Smoothing amount and Corner scale settings till you get the effect you want. (Don't forget you can save your settings as a preset for later reuse.)*

1 Choose Selections, Modify, Select Selection Borders

2 Choose a placement

3 Tinker with the Border width setting till you get the effect you need

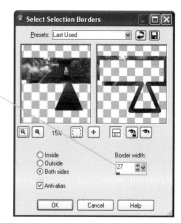

4 Click OK

5 The result – the bordered selection, ready for filling

# Vector selections

To select vector objects you've already created, carry out the following procedure.

## Selecting vector objects via the mouse

Click the Object
Selection tool in the
Tools palette

*To deselect all selections you've already made, press Ctrl+D.*

*You can also use the Object Selection tool to move vector objects. Click the object's outline (not its bounding box). Keep the pointer on the outline until it becomes a four-pronged arrow. Drag the object to a new location.*

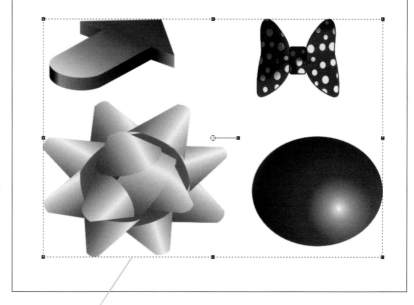

2 Click a single vector object (or its outline) or drag out a marquee around multiple objects

3 To remove a vector object from a selection group, hold down Ctrl as you left-click it

## Selecting vector objects via the Layer palette

*This is Paint Shop Pro 9's version of the Layers palette. Studio's palette is very slightly different.*

1 If the Layer palette isn't docked on the right of the screen, press the F8 key

2 Hold down Shift and click each object's layer name button

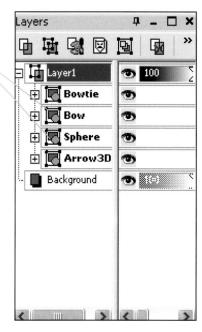

3 Here, Studio has selected the bow and sphere vectors

*Layers are a powerful editing tool which can take your use of Paint Shop Pro to a much higher level.*

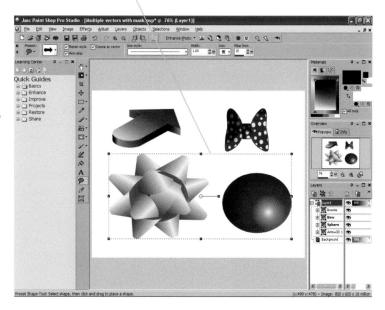

# Grouping/ungrouping

Paint Shop Pro lets you organize vector objects into "groups". When grouped, objects can be manipulated jointly in the normal way (for instance, you can save/load them.)

*Grouping vectors automatically moves them to the same layer.*

*You can have groups within groups. This is called "nesting".*

*To remove just one vector object from a group, drag its entry in the palette to a new layer or group.*

## Grouping vector objects

1 First select all the relevant vector objects (see pages 56–57 for how to do this)

2 Pull down the Objects menu and click Group

3 Or refer to the Layers palette. Hold down Shift and click the objects you want to group. Then right-click one and select Group in the menu

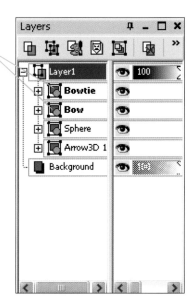

## Ungrouping vector objects

1 Select the group

2 Pull down the Objects menu and click Ungroup

3 Or, in the Layers palette, right-click the group name layer and select Ungroup

# Painting, drawing and text

In this chapter, you'll use paint/draw techniques with digital photographs. You'll perform freehand painting (including with Art Media tools); copy and substitute colors; select specific colors for foreground/background use; retouch images; spray-paint; fill images with colors, patterns, images, gradients and textures; and paint with object collections (picture tubes). You'll also create your own brush tips and get rid of backgrounds. Finally, you'll format and insert text (horizontal and vertical); create lines and preset shapes; then reshape them.

## Covers

**Chapter Three**

# Painting with the Paint Brush tool

*You can paint with the Warp brush, too, for some really cool effects.*

## Creating a painting

1 Click here in the Tool palette then click Paint Brush (or just hit B) – Studio has no Airbrush option

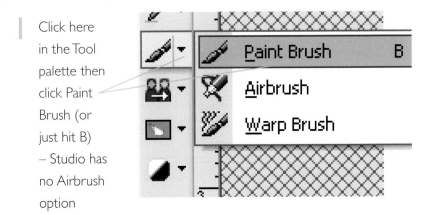

*If your Tool Options palette is floating, it'll likely look rather different. This book uses both docked and floating examples.*

2 If the Tool Options palette isn't onscreen, right-click the Tool Palette and select Palettes, Tool Options (or just hit F4)

3 Consider selecting a brush preset and/or brush tip then complete the Shape, Size, Hardness and Density fields. Experiment till you get the effects you want

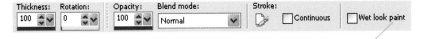

4 Complete the remaining settings, as appropriate – the Wet Look Paint one is really neat

**5** Drag with the left mouse button to paint with the active foreground color/materials or with the right mouse button to paint with the active background color/materials

**6** Experiment with presets for some interesting effects

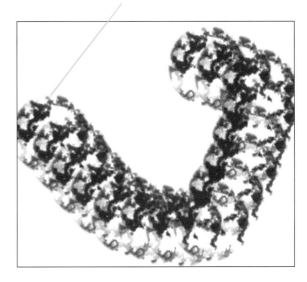

## Using the Brush Variance palette

If you're using Paint Shop Pro 9, once you've set brush options in steps 3–5, you can customize painting even further with the Brush Variance palette.

**1** Press the F11 key

**2** Click in each field and make a choice. Especially, experiment with 3 options at the base of the dialog box (Position jitter randomizes output)

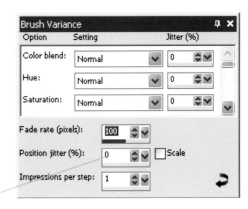

**3** Begin painting

*Why save brush tips when you can already save brush presets? Good question. The answer is that you can use brush tips with any brush tool (obviously, this includes the Paint and Airbrush tools, but also less obvious ones like the Retouch tools and the Background Eraser) while presets are tool-specific.*

## Customized brush tips

You can create you own brush tips for later reuse:

1 To convert an image area into a brush tip, just select it

2 Alternatively, select any brush tool in the Tool palette then adjust its settings in the Tool Options palette

3 Click here

4 Select Create brush tip or Create brush tip from selection, as appropriate

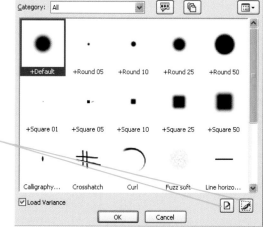

5 Complete the dialog then hit OK

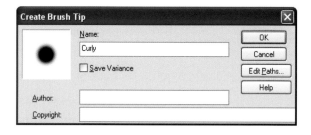

# Real-world painting Paint Shop Pro 9 only

Paint Shop Pro 9 has a series of Art Media tools which allow you to simulate the experience of working with what Jasc describes as "physical pigment media". These include paint, chalk, pastel and pencil. When you use these tools, Paint Shop Pro automatically inserts a new art media layer.

These tools fall into two broad categories: Wet Pigment Media (Oil Brush and Marker) and Dry Pigment Media (Chalk, Pastel, Crayon and Colored Pencil). The Wet Pigment tools tend to "run out" of paint – to replenish your brush, release the mouse button and then start to drag again.

There are also additional, specialized brushes:

- Palette Knife – use this to mimic an artist smearing pigments with a hard edge

- Smear – this reproduces the effect of smearing with a finger or cloth

- Art Eraser – use this to erase pigments

## Using the Art Media tools

1 Click here in the Tool palette

2 Select a brush

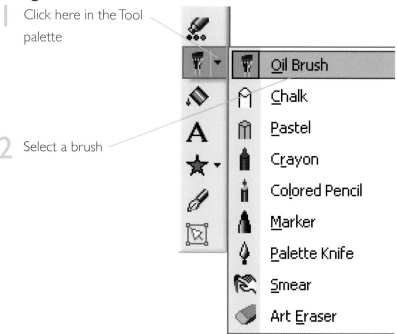

3 Customize your brush with the Tool Options palette (F4)

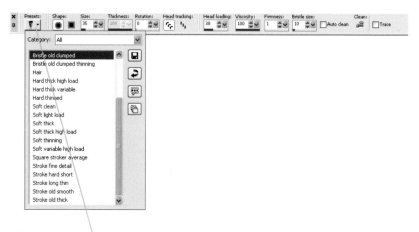

4 In particular, click the Presets button for a comprehensive list of brush presets – it's well worth looking to see if a preset exists that is close to the effect you want to achieve

5 Paint with the selected tool

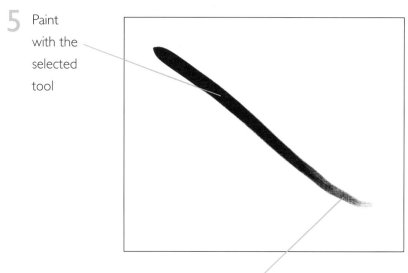

6 This is the Oil Brush – note that, characteristically, the paint is beginning to run out

## Using the Mixer palette

You can use a special palette to simulate an artist's palette. Use the Mixer palette to mix colors till you find the one you need then use any of the Art Media brushes to paint with it.

1 Launch the Mixer palette by pressing the Shift+F6 keys

2 Refer to the Materials palette and set the first foreground/stroke color you want to use. (Note, however, that the Mixer palette will not allow you to work with textures, patterns or gradient fills)

*You can undo the application of the last color by clicking the Unmix icon at the base of the palette.*

3 Select the Mixer Tube tool by clicking on this icon

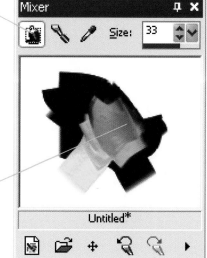

4 Paint with the color inside the palette

5 Select another color in the Materials palette and paint with this. Ensure the colors meet and then watch them form new colors

6 When you've gotten the color you want to paint with, activate the Mixer Dropper by clicking this icon:

7 Use this to promote the new color into the Materials palette

8 Activate one of the Art Media tools (see pages 63–64) and paint with your new color

# Copying with the Clone brush

*Cloning is extremely useful when you're working with photographs: use it to replace unwanted colors with colors that are desirable.*

Cloning is the copying of color from one location within an image to another (or to another image which has the same number of colors). To clone colors, you use the Clone brush.

### Cloning

Refer to the Tool palette and do the following:

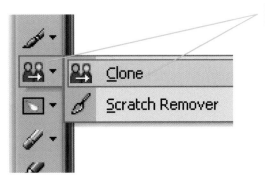

1 Click here in the Tool palette then click Clone (or just press C)

2 If the Tool Options palette isn't onscreen, right-click the Tool Palette and select Palettes, Tool Options (or just hit F4)

*Remember you can save Clone presets for reuse later.*

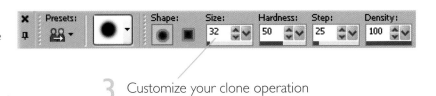

3 Customize your clone operation

4 Complete the remaining settings, too, as appropriate. Experiment till you achieve the effect you need

5 Place the mouse pointer over the image section you want to copy

6 Right-click once

7 Position the cursor where you want the paste operation to take place, then drag repeatedly

8 Crosshairs – these indicate the pixel which is currently being copied. As you drag in step 7, the crosshairs move, so you can select (on-the-fly) the area being copied

# Replacing color globally Paint Shop Pro 9 only

You can have Paint Shop Pro 9 replace a specified color with another. You do this by nominating the color you want to replace as the foreground color, then selecting the new color as the background color. (Or vice versa.)

You can replace colors globally (within an image or selection area) or manually (by using the Color Replacer tool as a brush).

### Carrying out a global substitution

Optional – if you want to limit the color exchange to a selected area, define a selection area

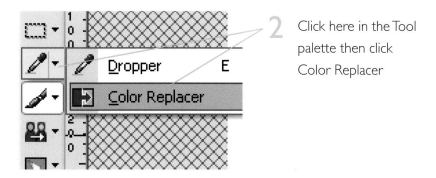

2 Click here in the Tool palette then click Color Replacer

3 If the Tool Options palette isn't onscreen, right-click the Tool Palette and select Palettes, Tool Options (or just hit F4)

*Tolerance settings are especially important with the Color Replacer. Low settings ensure that only pixels whose color is very similar will be changed. Increase the Tolerance settings to broaden the effect.*

4 Customize your color replace operation:

5 Remember you can save replace presets for reuse later

6 Double-click the left mouse button to replace the background with the foreground color

7 Alternatively, double-click the right mouse button to replace the foreground with the background color

8 Before ...

9 After – the color in the saucer (and part of the cup) has been replaced with white

# Replacing colors manually

## Creating a manual substitution

*More expensive programs like Adobe Photoshop have a color replacement feature but Paint Shop Pro's is arguably a lot easier to use.*

1 Create a selection area if you want to limit the replacement

2 Fire up the Color Replacer tool

3 Customize the Color Replacer tool till it works exactly the way you want it to

4 Drag with the left mouse button to replace the background with the foreground color or with the right to replace the foreground with the background color

*You can also use the Color Replacer to substitute colors as you create lines. Just left- or right-click (as appropriate) where you want the line to begin then hold down Shift and click somewhere else. Repeat as often as required.*

*Using the Color Replacer manually, it's especially important to get the right brush. Experiment and have fun!*

# Using the Dropper tool

The Dropper is an extremely useful tool which you can use to:

1.  select a color in the active image

2.  nominate this as the active foreground color or background color

## Using the Dropper

*A great timesaver – you can activate the Dropper within most paint tools by holding down Ctrl.*

Click here in the Tool palette then click Dropper. Or just press E (not D – that's the Deform tool)

3   The makeup of the color selected in step 2 displays in a fly-out:

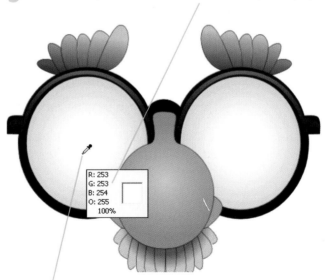

R: 253
G: 253
B: 254
O: 255
100%

*After step 3, the selected color appears in the Materials palette.*

2   Click with the left mouse button to nominate the selected color as the foreground or with the right to nominate it as the background

# Retouching – an overview

You can use the various Retouch tools to perform photo-retouching operations on images (or selected areas). These operations include:

### Burn
Darkens images.

### Dodge
Lightens image shadow.

*In Studio, Push and Emboss are not available as retouch tools.*

### Emboss
Produces a raised (stamped) effect in which the foreground is emphasized over the background.

### Push
This works like Smudge (see the entry below) but without picking up any color.

### Sharpen
The effect of this is obvious but it works by emphasizing edges and accentuating contrast. Many photographs benefit from the judicious application of this effect.

### Smudge
Produces a stained, blurred effect.

### Soften
Mutes the image (or selection) and diminishes contrast.

All the above tools (excluding Dodge and Burn) work with images which are 24 bit (16 million colors) or grayscale; the remainder work only with 24 bit images.

As a rule, you can't perform retouching operations globally. There is, however, one exception: Embossing. You achieve this via a special effect.

# Retouching images manually

## Carrying out a manual retouch operation

*You can also use the Retouch tools to retouch images by defining lines. Just left-click where you want the line to begin then hold down Shift and click somewhere else. Repeat as often as required.*

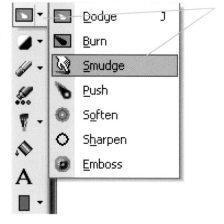

Click here in the Tool palette then select a retouch tool

*Different retouch tools have different options in the Tool Options palette. Try them all out.*

2 In the Tool Options palette (F4), customize your retouch operation e.g. select a preset if you've saved any and/or specify Size, Hardness, Density, Thickness and Opacity settings

3 Using a light touch, Shift+drag over the relevant area

*Here, an Emboss retouching operation is being carried out.*

# Using the Background Eraser

The new Background Eraser tool is a great way to get rid of image backgrounds while isolating the element of the picture you want to keep (often a person).

1   If the background you want to erase is on the Background layer, hit Layers, Promote Background Layer

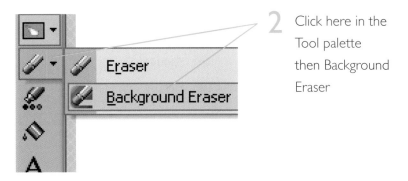

2   Click here in the Tool palette then Background Eraser

*You can save Background Eraser presets for reuse later.*

3   Customize your output in the Tool Options palette (F4) for example:

- Leave Auto tolerance checked initially. Later, uncheck it and enter a manual Tolerance setting – it's possible that this may produce a better effect

- If you want to replace the background with the foreground or background color/materials, select BackSwatch or ForeSwatch in the Sampling box

- Try reducing the Step size when you increase the Size setting – doing this can increase the rate at which the background is replaced

Because it intelligently senses where edges are, the Background Eraser tool does a lot of the work for you. However, you'll still have to spend some time making sure it hasn't missed any background.

4 Drag with the left mouse button near the picture's edge

5 The picture now has a transparent background

Zoom in with a small Size setting to tidy up around image edges. Then "mop up" the remainder of the background by zooming out, using a larger Size setting and holding down the Spacebar as you drag.

# Using the Airbrush tool

You can use the Airbrush tool to simulate painting with a spray can. You can do this in two ways.

## Using the Airbrush as a brush

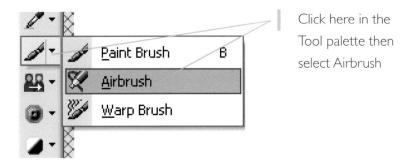

Click here in the Tool palette then select Airbrush

2   If the Tool Options palette isn't onscreen, right-click the Tool Palette and select Palettes, Tool Options (or just hit F4)

3   Complete all these additional fields, as appropriate

*Remember you can save Airbrush presets for reuse later.*

4   Complete the remaining settings, too, as appropriate. The Rate box is especially important for the Airbrush tool because it determines the rate at which paint is applied (range: 0–50). "0" applies an even quantity of paint while higher values apply more when you drag slowly or pause

5   Hold down the left mouse button then drag to paint with the active foreground color/materials

6   Alternatively, hold down the right mouse button then drag to paint with the active background color/materials

*This Airbrush uses the Marble3 brush tip with the Rate setting at 5 and the Blend Mode setting at Normal – the color is set to red.*

### Using the Airbrush to draw lines

1   Fire up the Airbrush tool then customize it till it works exactly the way you want it to

2   Click where you want the Airbrush operation to begin then hold down Shift and click where you want the line segment to end

3   Repeat for as many extra line segments as you want to insert

# Filling with colors

You can use the Flood Fill tool to fill a selection or image layer with color/materials (e.g. gradients). You can also fill with a specific image you've already opened into an additional window – this can produce some unique and fun effects.

## Filling images with a color

1 If you want to limit the effect of your fill, select part of the picture

2 Click the Flood Fill tool in the Tool palette

3 If the Tool Options palette isn't onscreen, right-click the Tool Palette and select Palettes, Tool Options (or just hit F4)

*Remember you can save Flood Fill tool presets for reuse later.*

4 Customize your flood fill operation for example:

- Blend mode – all options except Normal ensure that the fill is affected by the underlying image colors

- Match Mode – determine how Paint Shop Pro decides which pixels are covered (None covers all pixels)

- Opacity (range: 1–100)

- Tolerance – enter a value in this range: 0 (only exact matches are filled) to 200 (every pixel is filled)

5 Left-click to insert the foreground color OR right-click to insert the background color

*In effect, because they both target pixels that fulfill specific color criteria, the Flood Fill tool is similar to the Color Replacer tool. The main difference, however, is that Flood Fill operations affect contiguous pixels whereas color replacement operations generally target pixels in the whole layer.*

6 This is a preset gradient – *Blue neon*

# Filling with images

You can use the Materials palette to apply images to other images.

### Filling an image with another

1 Open the 16-million-color or grayscale image you want to insert

2 Now open the 16-million-color or grayscale image you want to insert it into

3 Activate the Flood Fill tool and customize it in the usual way

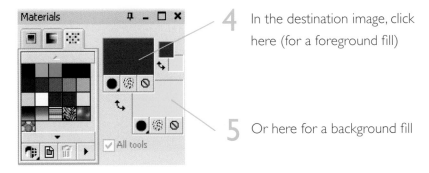

4 In the destination image, click here (for a foreground fill)

5 Or here for a background fill

6 Select the Pattern tab then click in Current Pattern to select the fill image. Finally, click OK

*Want to add a texture to colors, gradients or patterns? Check Texture on the right of the dialog then click in the box below and select a texture. Customize the texture till you get it the way you want.*

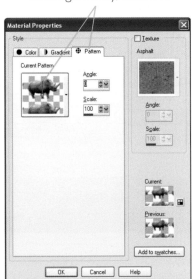

7 In the destination image, left-click to insert the foreground color/
materials or right-click to insert the background color/materials

# Filling with gradients

*Select image areas before applying the gradient to limit its effect.*

Gradient fills can look spectacularly effective.

1 Open the 16-million-color or grayscale image you want to fill

2 Carry out steps 3–5 on page 80

*To customize the gradient even more, click the Edit button then specify lighting and transparency settings.*

3 Select the Gradient tab

4 Click here and select a gradient in the list

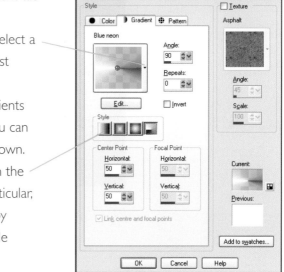

5 The preset gradients are great but you can customize your own. Experiment with the settings – in particular, vary the effect by changing the style

*Additional tools with which you can apply gradients include the Paint Brush, Clone, Color Replacer and Airbrush tools.*

6 Left- or right-click repeatedly in the image to insert the gradient

# Inserting patterns

1. Open the 16-million-color or grayscale image you want to fill

2. Carry out steps 3–5 on page 80

3. Select the Pattern tab

4. Click here and select a pattern

5. Customize the Angle and Scale settings

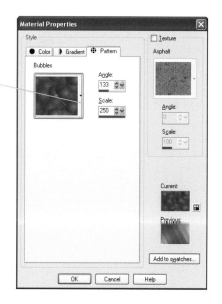

6. Left- or right-click repeatedly in the image to insert the pattern

# Inserting text with the Text tool

You can insert three principal types of text:

## Vector

This can only be created on a vector layer. Vector text is actually a vector object and can thus be edited, moved and deformed. (It can also be added to paths.)

## Floating (raster)

This appears above the current layer.

## Selection

This is an empty, transparent selection that can be filled.

1  Click the Text tool in the Tool palette (or press T)

2  Use the Materials palette to select a foreground color (the text outline) and a background color (the text fill) in the usual way

3  If the Tool Options palette isn't onscreen, right-click the Tool Palette and select Palettes, Tool Options (or just hit F4)

4  Select a text type, font and type size by clicking in the appropriate box and making a choice from the drop-down list

5  Select a font style – options vary with the typeface selected

*Auto kern adjusts the gaps between letters, so text looks better. Leading is the gap between lines.*

6 Select one of the many line styles then complete the remaining fields – for example, check Auto kern or specify a leading/tracking

7 Click where you want the text inserted

*Want text with a colored border? Use the Materials palette to select a foreground color before you create the text, then enter a Stroke width value in the Tool Options palette.*

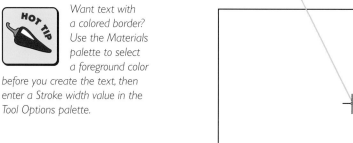

8 Enter your text and watch it appear onscreen. (Need a line break? Just press Enter)

*You can use the dialog on the right to apply text formatting. Just highlight text then make changes in the Tool Options palette – however, the changes don't show up in the dialog, just onscreen.*

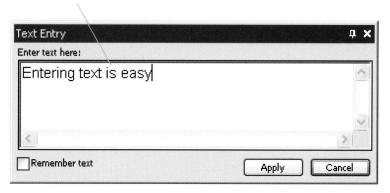

# Editing text

*To resize, rotate or distort vector text, you can use the Object Selection tool.*

1 To edit inserted vector text, place the Text tool mouse pointer over the text and left-click

2 Change and/or reformat the text in the Text Entry dialog

3 Alternatively, you can use the Layer palette. Press the F8 key if it isn't visible

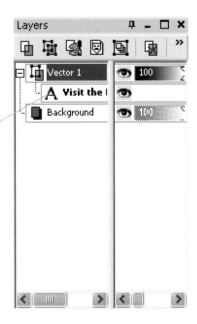

4 Double-click the relevant text layer (shown by "A" to the left) to launch the Text Entry dialog box

# Advanced text use

## Text and vectors

1 You can insert vector text onto vector object outlines or open paths (open paths have start and end points)

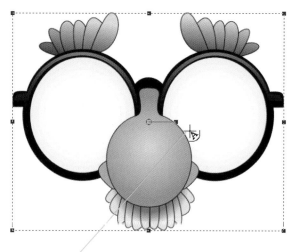

2 With the Text tool active, move the mouse pointer over the relevant vector object (as here) or path until the cursor changes

3 Ensure you've selected Vector (and an alignment) in the Tool Options palette

4 Click the outline or path then complete the Text Entry dialog

5 Click Apply in the dialog to confirm

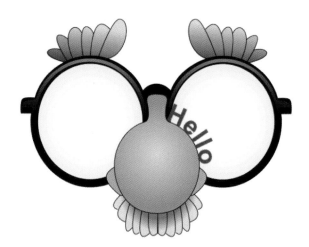

## Vertical text

You can insert vertical text in Paint Shop Pro 9. You can do this
with two orientations: "Vertical and left" and "Vertical and right".

*You can insert
vertical text in
Studio, too.*

1  Launch the Text tool by pressing T

2  Use the Materials palette to select a foreground color (the text
   outline) and a background color (the text fill) in the usual way

3  If the Tool Options palette isn't onscreen, right-click the Tool
   Palette and select Palettes, Tool Options (or just press F4)

4  Set standard text parameters in the normal way

5  Click here and select a vertical text option from the list

6  Create the
   text in the
   usual way

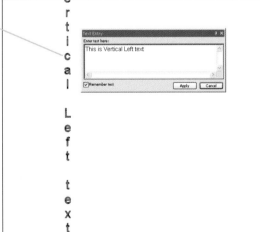

# Drawing with the Pen tool

Paint Shop Pro has a separate tool which you can use to create more detailed lines/curves.

### Drawing single lines

1 Click the Pen tool in the Tool palette. Or just hit V (not P – that's the Preset Shapes tool)

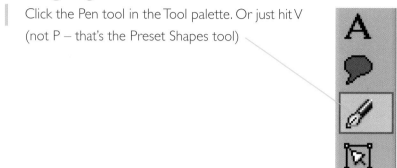

2 Select this to draw standard lines

3 Customize your output in the Tool Options palette (F4). For example, click in the Line Style field and select a style. Enter a line width in the Width: field (range: 1–255). Select Create On Vector (for a fully editable line)

4 Drag with the left mouse button to draw the line

5 Click the Apply button in the palette

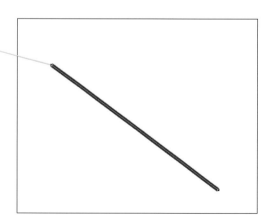

## Drawing single lines with multiple segments

1 Activate the Pen tool

2 Select this and check Connect Segments

3 Customize your output in the Tool Options palette above (F4)
– see page 89 for suggestions

4 Left-click to start then click elsewhere to begin new line segments

*If you create three nodes without clicking Apply, Paint Shop Pro treats the new lines as a single object and fills it (as here) with the background color/materials.*

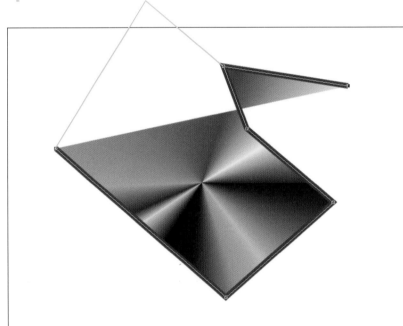

5 Click the Apply button in the palette

## Drawing Freehand lines

1　Activate the Pen tool

2　Select this and check Connect Segments

3　Customize your output in the Tool Options palette above (F4)

4　Drag with the left mouse button. The line itself is drawn with the foreground color/materials and any fill (as below) with the background color/materials

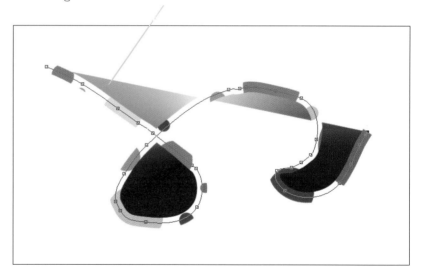

5　Click the Apply button in the palette

### Drawing Bézier curves

1 Follow steps 1–3 on page 89

2 Drag with the left mouse button to define the curve's length then release the button

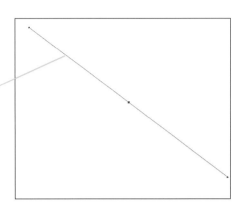

3 Drag elsewhere to create a curve then release the button

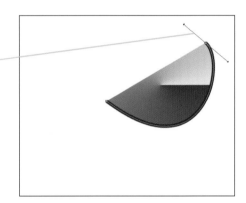

4 Repeat for as many curves as you need

5 Click the Apply button in the palette

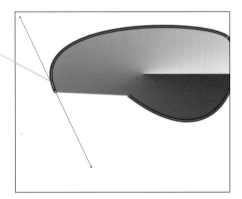

# Using the Picture Tube tool

You can also paint using object collections called "picture tubes". When you do this, Paint Shop Pro automatically inserts a variety of related objects.

## Painting with the Picture Tube tool

*Picture Tubes only work with raster layers. Also, images must be grayscale or 16-million colors.*

**1** Click the Picture Tube tool in the Tool palette. Or just hit I

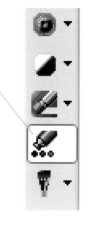

*Paint Shop Pro 9 users can create their own tubes, using the File, Export, Picture Tube command – the procedure is straightforward. For more information, press F1 to launch Help then search for the "Creating Picture Tubes" topic.*

**3** Select a tube then this:

*Remember you can save Picture Tube presets for reuse later.*

**2** Customize your output in the Tool Options palette (F4) e.g.:

- set the tube size in the Scale field (range: 10%–250%)

- increase the Step setting to give less contact between the brush tip and the image surface (this makes the tube's outline more prominent, and the stroke less dense)

*Available Picture Tubes vary in Paint Shop Pro 9 and Studio.*

- Placement mode – select Random (objects appear at random intervals) or Continuous (equal intervals)

- Selection mode – select Random (objects are chosen haphazardly); Incremental (objects are inserted one at a time); Angular (objects appear according to painting direction); or Velocity (objects appear according to painting speed)

*Want more picture tubes? You can get them free at www.jasc.com and elsewhere on the Internet.*

4 You optionally can customize cell arrangement details with this dialog box:

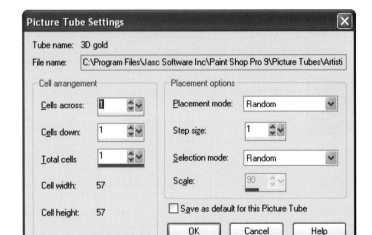

*You can get your version tubes from earlier versions to work with Paint Shop Pro 9/Studio but you need a special converter. Go to www4. jasc.com/pub/tubcnvrt.exe.*

5 Drag with the left mouse button and/or click repeatedly

*Adjust the various settings to vary the impact – the effect can be quite marked.*

# Drawing with preset shapes

You can create shapes (e.g. rectangles, stars and symbol-based vectors like arrows, circles and stars).

*The procedures described here work with Paint Shop Pro 9. With Studio, however, you can only select one vector tool: the Preset Shape Tool.*

1 Click this icon in the Tool palette

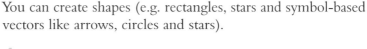

2 Select the appropriate tool

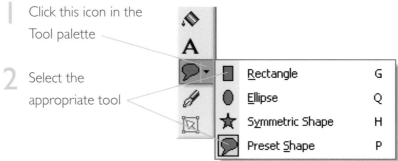

*In Paint Shop Pro 9, when you've used the Rectangle tool (G) to create a rectangle, you can give it rounded corners. Press O then double-click the rectangle. In the Vector Property dialog, click the Join box and select the appropriate option.*

4 Click here

3 Customize your output in the Tool Options palette (F4). The options vary according to which tool you chose in step 2 – these are the settings for the Preset Shape tool. Whichever choices you make, ensure that Create as vector is checked for optimal editability

*Select Create as vector to define a vector shape, or deselect this to create a raster one instead.*

5 Select a shape

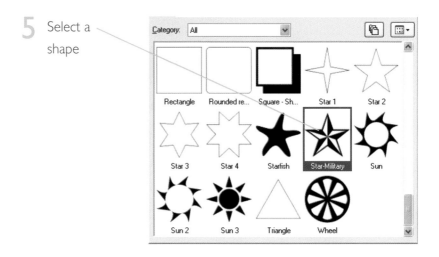

*To draw from the center outwards, drag with the right mouse button. To draw proportionately, hold down Shift.*

*With Paint Shop Pro 9, vector shapes can be edited at any time, even after you've completed the graphic.*

6 Drag with the left mouse button to draw the shape

7 Uncheck Retain style in the Tool Options palette if you want the shape's line to follow the foreground color/materials, or its fill to follow the background color/materials

# Editing preset shapes

1 Click the Object Selection tool in the Tool palette. Or just hit O

2 Right-click the selected vector and hit Properties

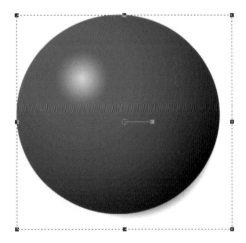

*You can also customize vector placement, alignment and distribution in the Tool Options palette.*

3 Complete the dialog fields. For example, to amend the shape width, enter a new entry in the Stroke width field. Or, to apply a new fill, make sure Fill is checked then click in the box below and select a new one

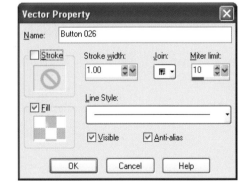

# Node editing – an overview

Vector objects use a hierarchy. Each object contains one path. Each path consists of at least one contour. Each contour has at least one straight or curved segment and two or more nodes (they determine object shape) and can be open or – as here – closed.

The ability to edit nodes in Paint Shop Pro means you can produce some unique effects.

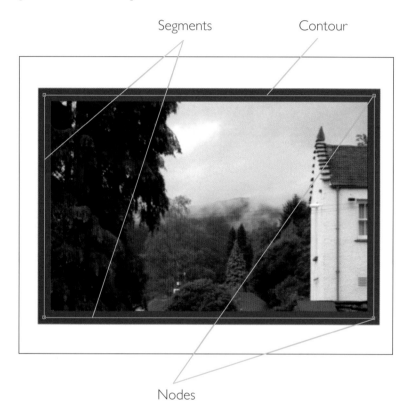

Segments    Contour

Nodes

Editing (manipulating) nodes is carried out in a special mode called Edit Mode. This:

-  displays the vector's path

-  does not accurately reflect the vector's true appearance

Only one path can be edited at once, but you can use nodes to reshape vector objects in an almost infinite number of ways.

# Selecting nodes

1 If the Pen tool isn't active, hit V

2 In the Tool Options palette, select the Edit Mode icon:

3 Select a node for editing

4 Or drag out a marquee to select multiple nodes

# Node operations

## Adding new nodes

Follow steps 1–2 on the previous page then:

1 Hold down Ctrl as you left-click a contour

*The effect of moving a node depends on its type – see the facing page for more information.*

## Moving nodes

Follow steps 1–2 on the previous page then:

1 Select one or more nodes

*Dragging a segment rather than a node moves the entire contour.*

2 Drag the node(s) to a new location

*Paint Shop Pro has various node types. Smooth nodes allow curves and lines to blend smoothly. Cusp nodes produce marked directional changes. Symmetric and Asymmetric nodes both give a smooth flow through the node but in Symmetric the result is more harmonious.*

## Changing a node's type

Applying a new type to a node has an impact on the segments which enter and leave it.

In Node Edit mode, right-click a node. Select Node Type then click a type

## Merging nodes

When you "merge" a node, you delete it. This results in the two segments which enter it being united into one.

In Edit Mode, select 1 or more nodes

*Merging every node within a contour deletes the contour.*

2 Press Ctrl+M – the result can be unexpected

## Breaking nodes

You can "break" nodes. This means that the contour in which the node is situated is split into two separate contours (if the original was open) or opened out (if the original contour was closed).

1 In Node Edit mode, left-click a node

2 Press Ctrl+K then drag the nodes apart

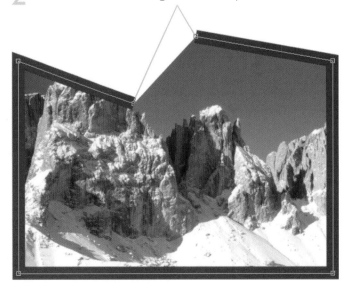

# Filters

In this chapter, you'll learn how to add a variety of creative effects to images or image selections. You'll do this by applying any of Paint Shop Pro's numerous filters.

Finally, you'll create your own filters and save these as presets.

## Covers

**Chapter Four**

# Using filters

*The distinction between filters, deformations and effects is sometimes less than precise.*

Paint Shop Pro provides numerous effects that you can use to enhance your photographs etc. Effects are organized under various categories. Filters are specialized effects that, generally speaking, enhance images or image selections by varying the color of every pixel ("picture element") in line with its current color and the colors of any neighboring pixels.

You can also create and apply your own filters, for some really distinctive and original effects.

## Applying a filter

*Many filters only work with images with 16-million colors or more (if they have fewer colors, press Ctrl+Shift+0) and 256-color grayscales.*

1 Optionally, pre-select part of the relevant image or select a layer in the Layers palette

2 Pull down the Effects menu and click Effect Browser

*Paint Shop Pro 9 has more filters than Studio.*

3 Select Effects, Edge Effects in the tree

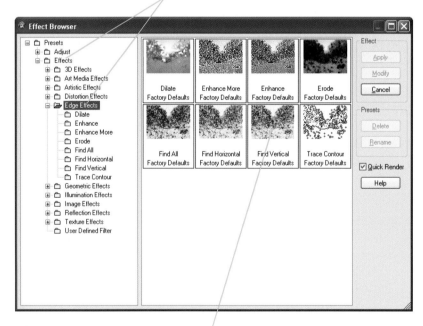

4 Double-click a filter preview to apply it (or select one then click Modify to customize it)

# Filter Gallery

Paint Shop Pro ships with numerous filters. Some of the most useful are detailed in this chapter.

*Applying the same filter more than once can often give superior results.*

*There's a handy shortcut you can use to do this in Paint Shop Pro 9 (but not Studio): just press Ctrl+Y.*

Compare this unchanged image with subsequent examples

## Sample filters

*The Dilate filter enhances light areas in an image.*

Dilate

*Entries in brackets represent presets.*

Enhance

*Use the Enhance More filter (it works by amplifying edge contrast) to increase image clarity. (For a similar but reduced effect, use the Enhance filter.)*

Enhance
More

*Erode emphasizes edges by applying a stronger contrast to them.*

Erode

*The Trace Contour filter is a specialist edge filter which, effectively, outlines images by defining a border around them. (The Find Horizontal, Find Vertical and Find All filters produce similar results but with slightly different emphases.)*

Trace
Contour

## Additional filters

You'll also find filters in the Adjust section of the Effect Browser.

*Use Add Noise (in moderation) to remove imperfections from images.*

Add Noise

*Paint Shop Pro offers more specialized filters. For example, use the Deinterlace filter to correct video images. Use the Despeckle filter to blur all of an image except those locations (edges) where meaningful color changes take place.*

Automatic
Color Balance
(Strong warm)

*Use the Average filter to remove noise which is spread over the whole of an image. (This filter is also useful with pictures whose color depth you've increased.)*

Average
(Blur Medium)

*Scanned in JPEG images? You'll likely find they have "artifacts", unwanted color leakage or blocky-looking colors. Use the JPEG Artifact Removal filter to correct this problem. If this doesn't work, try the Moiré Pattern Removal filter.*

Curves
(Intense
Primaries)

*Displacement Map creates custom 2- or 3-dimensional surface effects.*

Displace-
ment Map
(Jumble
black)

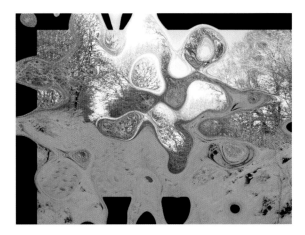

*Use Hue Map as a way to change one or more colors in complex photographs, or to make them lighter.*

Hue Map
(Neon
Glow)

*Paint Shop Pro offers numerous filters you can use to change ("correct") colors in photographs, and this is just one of them. The presets (such as Underwater) are certainly well worth exploring.*

Manual Color Correction (Underwater)

*Photographs tend to acquire "noise", specks of unwanted color that impose a grainy effect. Paint Shop Pro provides various filters designed to eliminate noise. Use Median Filter to remove small areas of noise which are distinct from surrounding areas.(See also Salt and Pepper.)*

Median Filter (Filter high)

*Motion Blur makes an image look as though it was moving when the photograph was taken. Use the Motion Blur dialog to specify a strength and angular direction.*

Motion Blur (Double vision)

*Not a corrective technique, Radial Blur simulates the effect of zooming in with a very low shutter speed.*

Radial Blur

*Use the Salt and Pepper filter to remove noise/ specks (e.g. dust) from photographs. It works best when you apply it to a predefined selection.*

Salt and Pepper (Aggressive large)

*Sharpen and Sharpen More intensify contrast between contiguous pixels and thus improve image focus.*

Sharpen

Sharpen
More

*The Soft Focus
filters produce
results that are
close to a specific
camera filter.*

Soft Focus
(Halo large)

*Unsharp Mask is
the sharpening
filter preferred
by professionals.
It can produce
some pretty dramatic effects.
Paint Shop Pro provides various
– and quite unusual – presets.*

Unsharp
Mask (Edge
glow)

# Creating filters  Paint Shop Pro 9 only

You can easily define your own filters. Once created, new filters can be saved as presets.

*Click the Save icon on the top right of the dialog to save your filter as a preset.*

*Often (but not always), specifying lots of settings in the dialog will produce little or no effect. Generally, using fewer settings gives more visible results.*

1 Pull down the Effects menu and click User Defined Filter

2 Select a preset or enter your own filter parameters

3 Stuck for somewhere to start? Try clicking the Randomize button (you can also do this in any other modifiable filter) then manually amend the result

4 The original image on page 105 after applying a user-defined filter

# Deformations

In this chapter, you'll distort images or selections with specialized effects called deformations. Then you'll learn how to utilize additional manual techniques which are not only handy (you can use them to correct photographic misalignments), they're also fun (you can create some seriously warped effects with them).

## Covers

Chapter Five

# Deformations

*The distinction between filters, deformations and effects is sometimes less than precise.*

Deformations enhance images (or image selections, if you've pre-selected part of a picture) by transferring data from one image area to another. This makes them more spectacular than filters.

## Applying a deformation

1 Optionally, pre-select part of the relevant image or select a layer in the Layers palette

2 Pull down the Effects menu and click Effect Browser

3 Under Effects, select Distortion Effects or Geometric Effects

*Many deformations only work with images with 16-million colors or more (if they have fewer colors, press Ctrl+Shift+0) and 256-color grayscales.*

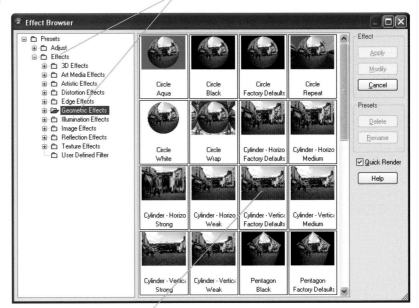

*Paint Shop Pro 9 has more deformations than Studio.*

4 Double-click a preview to apply it (or select one then click Modify to customize it)

5 Stuck for somewhere to start? Try hitting the Randomize (dice) button when you modify a deformation

# Deformation Gallery

Paint Shop Pro ships with numerous deformations. We demonstrate some of the most useful.

Compare this unchanged image with subsequent examples

## Sample deformations

Circle (Wrap)

Curlicues (Four by four)

*Applying either of the Cylinder distortions (Horizontal and Vertical) more than once can make your photograph unrecognizable.*

Cylinder Horizontal (Strong)

Lens Distortion (Fisheye offset)

*Self-explanatory, but you can achieve results which aren't just "straight" pentagons by varying the Edge mode setting when you customize the Pentagon deformation.*

Pentagon (Wrap)

*The Perspective Vertical deformation slants an image vertically. (The Perspective Horizontal deformation does the same, only horizontally.)*

Perspective Vertical (Streaks)

Pinch (Strong)

*When you customize this deformation, try varying the Edge mode setting.*

Polar Coordinates (Rectangular wrap)

*Punch imposes the opposite effect to Pinch.*

Punch (Strong)

*The Factory version of Ripple defines concentric rings around an image's midpoint. However, you can vary the start point, as here.*

Ripple (Big waves left)

*The Skew deformation slants images.*

Skew (with a minus Skew angle)

Spherize

*Spiky Halo applies a crown of waves arranged radially. This example shows how extreme the results of applying this deformation can be.*

Spiky Halo

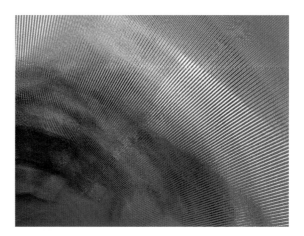

*The Twirl deformation rotates an image around its center.*

Twirl (Right 500)

*The Warp deformation magnifies an image's center in relation to the remainder. You can slant the effect, though, as here.*

Warp (Large Upper left)

*The Wave deformation imposes undulating vertical and horizontal lines – customizing this deformation can get pretty psychedelic.*

Wave

*Wind applies the effect of wind coming from the left or right.*

Wind

# The Deform tool

Paint Shop Pro 9 has various deformation techniques that you can use to correct digital photographs (or just to produce interesting and fun effects).

*If you define a selection, Paint Shop Pro will prompt you to promote it to a full layer. Hit OK in the dialog.*

## Deforming manually

1 Select the layer you want to deform (if you're working on the Background layer, promote it first – Layers, Promote Background Layer) or define a selection area, if appropriate

2 Click here in the Tool palette then click Deform. Or press D

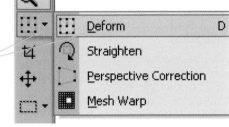

*Hold down Ctrl and Shift to distort the image. This is more for entertainment than image correction.*

3 Optionally, turn on the Grid to aid realignment (Ctrl+Alt+G)

4 Hold down Ctrl and drag a corner handle to edit the perspective

*Hold down Shift as you drag a central handle to skew the image.*

*Increase the Canvas size (Image, Canvas Size) if, as a result of using the Deform tool, any parts of the image are no longer visible.*

5 Or place the mouse pointer over the horizontal line – when the pointer changes to two circular arrows, drag to rotate

# The Perspective Correction tool

*If you define a selection, Paint Shop Pro will prompt you to promote it to a full layer. Hit OK in the dialog.*

You can also adjust image perspective more directly.

1 Select the layer you want to deform or define a selection area

2 Follow step 2 on page 121 but select Perspective Correction

3 Customize the correction in the Tool Options palette (F4)

*When you set parameters in the Tool Options palette, check Crop image to revert the image to its original size after the perspective has been changed. Optionally, enter a value in the Grid lines box to display a helpful grid. You can also fine-tune the bounding box position by entering values in the various X and Y boxes.*

4 A bounding box appears – drag the corners till the box defines an area which ought to be 100% straight

5 Double-click inside the box

*In the Tool Options palette, you can save Perspective Correction presets for reuse later.*

6 If the effect isn't quite what you want, press the Ctrl+Z keys. Vary the box position slightly then repeat the procedure – sometimes, only subtle changes are required when you use this tool

# The Straighten tool

You can straighten (or unstraighten) images by rotating them on-the-fly around a user-defined line.

1  Select the layer you want to deform or define a selection area

*This tool works best with images with strong vertical/horizontal components.*

2  Follow step 2 on page 121 but select Straighten

3  Customize the correction in the Tool Options palette (F4)

4  A straightening bar appears – drag the ends till the bar aligns with the image part you want to straighten

*Any portions of the image canvas exposed by the straightening operation are filled with the background color/pattern/texture.*

5  Double-click the image

*Increase the Canvas size (Image, Canvas Size) if this operation results in any parts of the image no longer being visible.*

6  If the effect isn't quite what you want, press the Ctrl+Z keys. Vary the bar position slightly then repeat step 5

# The Mesh Warp tool

You can warp images on-the-fly.

1 Select the layer you want to deform or define a selection area

2 Follow step 2 on page 121 but select Mesh Warp

3 In the Tool Options palette (F4), customize the mesh grid then check Best quality for a high-quality warp

*Use the Warp brush instead (see page 126) when you want to blend the area being warped with the remainder of the image.*

4 Drag one or more nodes to warp the picture – hold down Shift while you drag to move the entire row or column or Ctrl to create a smooth curve

## Using deformation maps

You can save details of the nodes and lines you've created with the Mesh Warp tool as special "deformation maps" and then apply these to other images.

1 After you've applied a mesh warp deformation, click the Save Deformation Map button in the Tool Options palette

2 Name the map then click the Save button

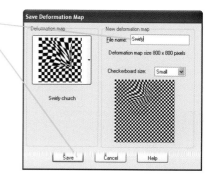

3 To apply the deformation map to a new image, load it then click the Open Deformation Map button in the palette

4 Complete the dialog box – specifically, select the map, choose a placement then pick a checkerboard size before clicking Load to apply the map:

# The Warp brush

You can also deform images with the use of a special Paint Shop Pro brush.

1 Click here in the Tool palette then click Warp Brush (this menu looks slightly different in Studio)

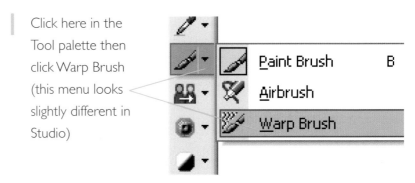

*There are several warp modes. Push performs a smearing action in the direction of the brush stroke. Expand pushes pixels out from the center. Right Twirl and Left Twirl rotate pixels around the brush's center. Noise moves pixels randomly under the brush. Use Iron Out and Unwarp to undo warps.*

2 Refer to the Tool Options palette (F4) then select a warp mode (check them out to see what they can do) and/or customize the remaining fields, especially Strength (range: 1–100)

3 Check Best quality for optimal results

*You can save Warp brush effects as deformation maps. See page 125 for how to do this.*

4 Make sure your Brush Variance settings are optimized

5 Drag over the image to deform it (this is Push)

# Effects and photographic corrections

In this chapter, you'll enhance images or image selections by applying any of numerous special effects. You'll also apply 3D effects to image selections, magnify sections with the Magnifying Lens and turn images into seamless patterns for use as Web backgrounds.

Finally, Paint Shop Pro 9 (and, to a lesser extent, Studio) has new, specialized effects which you can use to correct errors that commonly occur in digital photographs. You'll enhance photos with One Step Photo Fix, which oftentimes is all you'll need. When this isn't enough, you'll also resolve lighting deficiencies, remove scratches, eliminate moiré and correct red-eye.

## Covers

**Chapter Six**

# Using effects

Paint Shop Pro provides numerous special effects. These include artistic effects, texture effects, effects which apply or reflect light and additional effects that you can use to correct photographs.

## Applying an effect

1 Optionally, pre-select part of the relevant image or select a layer in the Layers palette

2 Pull down the Effects menu and click Effect Browser

*Many effects only work with images with 16-million colors or more (if they have fewer colors, press Ctrl+Shift+0) and 256-color grayscales.*

3 Under Effects, select an appropriate category (Art Media Effects, Artistic Effects, Image Effects, Illumination Effects, Reflection Effects or Texture Effects)

*Paint Shop Pro 9 has more effects than Studio.*

4 Double-click a preview to apply it (or select one then click Modify to customize it)

5 Stuck for somewhere to start? Try hitting the Randomize (dice) button when you modify a effect

# Effect Gallery

Paint Shop Pro ships with numerous effects. Some of the most useful are detailed in this chapter.

Compare this unchanged image with subsequent examples

## Sample effects

Aged Newspaper (100 years)

Balls and Bubbles (Reflecting globs)

*You can specify whether the blinds are horizontal or vertical.*

Blinds

*Brush Strokes makes images look like watercolors.*

Brush
Strokes

*Charcoal converts to black and white and then mimics the effect of being drawn with charcoal. If the Opacity setting is set to less than 100, some colors show thru. (The Black Pencil effect is similar but gives more detail.)*

Charcoal

*Chrome mimics applying a metallic patina to images.*

Chrome (Toxic)

*Colored Foil combines a sculpted look with multiple colors.*

Colored Foil (High blur)

*Contours changes images into topographical maps (see also "Topography").*

Contours (Busy red)

*Emboss transforms the image into a bas-relief (shapes project from the background without becoming detached). Colors are also inserted when appropriate. You can't customize Emboss.*

Emboss

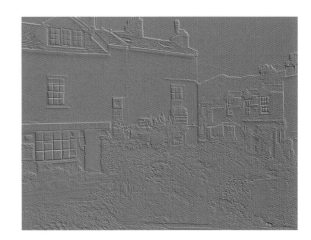

*Feedback makes an image appear to be reflected inwards in concentric mirrors.*

Feedback

Fur

Glowing
Edges
(Sharp and
intense)

 *Halftone turns photographs into dot representations. Using Randomize can get a little psychedelic, especially if Ink and Background colors are set.*

Halftone

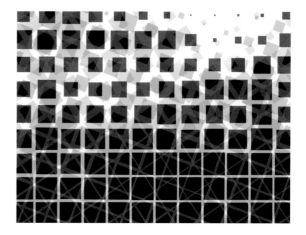

 *Kaleidoscope isolates a pie-shaped section and converts this into a circular pattern.*

Kaleidoscope

*Lights spotlights images – you can specify the number of spotlights. Explore the presets for useful effects.*

Lights (Christmas corners)

*Neon Glow makes images 3D and emphasizes edge contrast. Experiment with Randomize for wacky effects.*

Neon Glow (Extreme tint)

*This is the default Page Curl setting – try varying the curl and edge colors. You can also specify which corner curls.*

Page Curl

*Pencil – as well as making an image look like a pencil drawing – also colors the edges. Varying the Color setting can have dramatic results, as can using Randomize.*

Pencil
(Intense
red)

Posterize
(High
contrast)

*Vary the Color and Luminance settings especially till you get the result you want.*

Sandstone

Sculpture
(Deep
metal)

*Sepia Toning makes an image look as if it was produced in the 19th century – to achieve this, grayscale it (Image, Grayscale) then convert it to 16 million colors (Ctrl+Shift+0) before applying the effect. Or, to give the image a more modern, 1940s feel, apply Sepia Toning to a 16-million-color image.*

Sepia Toning
(Fully aged)

*Soft Plastic can get a little psychedelic, especially if you select a color and use a relative high Blur setting.*

Soft Plastic

*Solarize has unexpected applications. You can use it to convert photographs into negatives, and vice versa. For example, you could scan in a negative and then turn it into a photograph.*

Solarize (High)

*See page 140 for seamless tiling.*

Tiles

*Topography gives a 3D feel to an image. Again, Randomize can add a welcome flavor of exoticism.*

Topography

# The Magnifying Lens Paint Shop Pro 9 only

You can apply a lens to an image and magnify the area inside it. There are 47 lenses to choose from and, of course, you can easily create your own and save them as presets.

1 In the Effect Browser, select Effects, Artistic Effects, Magnifying Lens

2 Select a preset or the Factory Default

3 To fine-tune the lens, click Modify

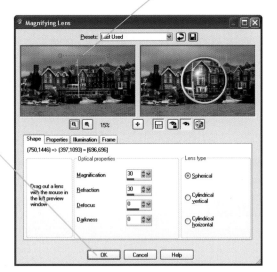

4 Use your mouse to resize and reposition the bounding box

5 Work your way thru the tabs, adjusting the various settings, then hit OK

*Drag in the right-hand Preview box to view the relevant image area. Click the Zoom In or Zoom Out icons to adjust the magnification.*

*There are also a few "user-defined" effects (under Effects/User Defined in the Browser), but not in Studio.*

6 Paint Shop Pro applies the lens – the above is the "Factory Default" preset. Hitting the Randomize button, however, can produce slightly different results, as below:

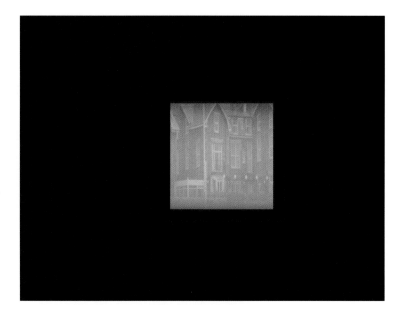

# Tiling effects

You can tile images seamlessly.

1 In the Effect Browser, select Effects, Image Effects, Seamless Tiling. Click an effect then hit Modify

2 Drag the "bullseye" to set the offset (point of origin) of the tiling effect

*Seamless tiles are especially effective as backgrounds in Web pages. Alternatively, apply them with the Flood Fill tool.*

3 Choose a tiling direction, method and corner style

4 Hit OK

5 This is the Seamless Tiling – "Factory Default" preset

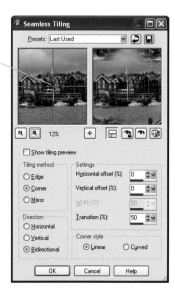

# 3D effects

Paint Shop Pro also ships with several neat 3D effects. These include Buttonize (very useful for websites), Chisel, Cutout and Drop Shadow.

## Applying a 3D effect

1 Some 3D effects only function if you've pre-defined a selection area. With these, press the Ctrl+A keys if you want to work on the whole of an image

2 In the Effect Browser, select Effects/3D Effects. Select a submenu e.g. Buttonize or Drop Shadow

3 Double-click an effect. This is Chisel (with the use of Randomize):

4 Or select an effect, click Modify then complete the dialog

# Correcting photographs

You can use a variety of specialist effects to enhance and correct photographs.

*One Step Photo Fix isn't a cure-all, however: you may still have to remove scratches or moiré.*

### One Step Photo Fix

1 Use One Step Photo Fix to adjust a raft of attributes, including color balance, contrast, clarity and saturation. It also smooths edges and sharpens the picture. Probably, 7 (or more) times out of 10, One Step Photo Fix will be all you need by way of correction

*Alternatively, use a manual approach. Select an individual option and complete any dialog.*

2 Click Enhance Photo in the Photo toolbar then One Step Photo Fix

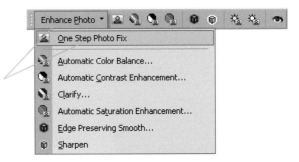

3 Before One Step Photo Fix

4 And after . . .

5 Try repeating One Step Photo Fix – the result may be even better

*Use Automatic Small Scratch Removal on images with reasonably smooth backgrounds.*

*Apply several times, watching carefully to make sure the remainder of the image doesn't suffer and fine-tuning the settings as required.*

Old photographs often have blemishes. Use the Automatic Small Scratch Removal tool to get rid of scratches.

## Scratch removal

1 Select Adjust, Add/Remove Noise, Automatic Small Scratch Removal

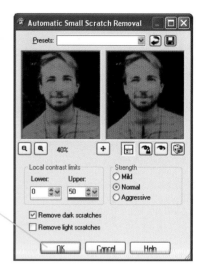

2 Complete the dialog then click OK

3 Before Automatic Small Scratch Removal

4 And after . . .

## Getting rid of moiré Paint Shop Pro 9 only

1 Moiré refers to undesirable patterns found principally on poorly scanned photographs. To get rid of moiré, choose Adjust, Add/Remove Noise, Moiré Pattern Removal

*First adjust the Fine details setting, then Remove bands. Take care, though: increasing these options too much can result in blurring.*

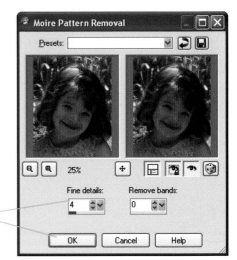

2 Complete the dialog then click OK

3 Before Moiré Pattern Removal

4 And after ...

5 After you've got rid of the unwanted moiré pattern, try (as here) running the Unsharp Mask filter on the image for greater clarity

## Flash Fill adjustments

1 Select Adjust, Photo Fix, Fill Flash

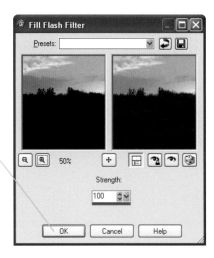

2 Complete the dialog then confirm the operation

3 Before Fill Flash. The camera has avoided overexposing the sky and, as a result, the foreground is way too dark

4 And after ...Try running Flash Fill repeatedly, as here

## Backlighting adjustments

1 Select Adjust, Photo Fix, Backlighting

2 Complete the dialog then confirm

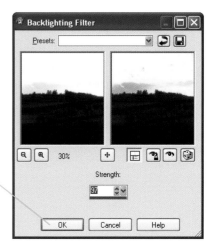

3 Before Backlighting. There is too much light from the background, and thus the rest of the image looks washed out

*Don't overdo backlighting adjustments.*

4 And after ...

## Chromatic Aberration **Paint Shop Pro 9 only**

*Digital cameras often insert incorrect colors into photographs – for example, when the sky is visible through branches, around the edges of backlit objects or when photographs contain illuminated light bulbs. Chromatic aberration is more likely when a zoom lens is used but can occur at any time.*

1 Select Adjust, Photo Fix, Chromatic Aberration

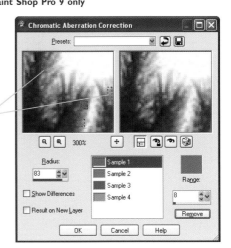

2 Zoom in then drag out boxes over instances of chromatic aberration

3 Complete the dialog then click OK

4 Notice the purplish cast to the leaves

5 And after ...

*It isn't just a case of eyes becoming red: they can acquire a variety of colors.*

## Removing red-eye

1  Select Adjust, Photo Fix, Red Eye Removal

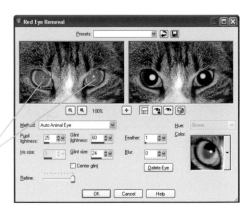

2  Select a method (Auto Human Eye or Auto Animal Eye) then, in the left window, click inside the eyes

3  Fine-tune the eyes till the result in the right window is suitable

4  Before red-eye removal

5  And after ...

# Getting images Web-ready

In this chapter, you'll learn how to customize and export images for use on the Web. Techniques you'll use include rollovers, slicing and mapping. You'll also send pictures by email directly from within Paint Shop Pro and upload them to free online sharing services such as Shutterfly, so other people can view and print them.

## Covers

**Chapter Seven**

# Image formats

Paint Shop Pro recognizes a wide selection of bitmap, vector and meta graphic formats. These are some of the main ones:

## Bitmap formats

PCX — Originated with PC Paintbrush. Used for years to transfer graphics data between Windows applications. Supports compression

TIFF — Tagged Image File Format. Suffix: .TIF. If anything, even more widely used than PCX, across a whole range of platforms and applications

BMP — Not as common as PCX and TIFF, but still popular

TGA — Targa. A high-end format, and also a bridge with so-called low-end computers (e.g. Amiga and Atari). Often used in PC and Mac paint and ray-tracing programs because of its high-resolution color fidelity

PCD — (Kodak) PhotoCD. Used primarily to store photographs on CD. Neither Paint Shop Pro nor Studio will export to PCD

GIF — Graphics Interchange Format. Just about any Windows program will read GIF. Frequently used on the Internet. Disadvantage: it can't handle more than 256 colors. Compression is supported

JPEG — Joint Photographic Experts Group. Used for photograph storage, especially on the Internet. It supports a very high-level of compression, usually without appreciable distortion

PNG — Interlaced Portable Network Graphics. Now widely used on the Internet

## Vector formats

CGM — Computer Graphics Metafile. Frequently used in the past, especially as a medium for clip-art transmission

EPS — The most widely used PostScript format. Combines vector and raster data with a low-resolution informational bitmap header

# Exporting images for the Web

You can use the File, Save As route (Chapter 1) to produce files suitable for Web use. However, there's a more convenient technique: you can use specialized export dialogs.

1 Select File, Export then select JPEG Optimizer, GIF Optimizer or PNG Optimizer

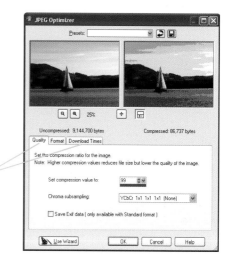

*Some PCs are limited to 256-color display. Images with more colors are "dithered" and are often distorted. As a result, it's a good idea to reduce images you create for the Web to 256 colors (Ctrl+Shift+3). Unfortunately, you can't do this in Studio.*

2 Click each tab then set the necessary options – these vary somewhat with the output format. With JPEG, for example, use Quality to specify compression (don't overdo it), Format to set the output format and Download Times to check your file will download in a reasonable time

3 This is the route for Internet gurus. If you want a simpler path to Web file creation, click the Use Wizard button in the above dialog

*Before you export a layered picture for Web use, flatten it by pulling down the Layers menu and selecting Merge, Merge All (Flatten).*

4 Work through the Wizard

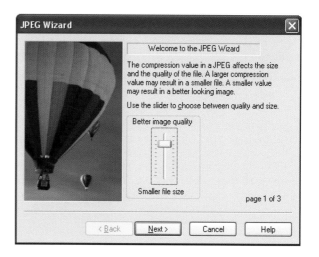

# Image slicing Paint Shop Pro 9 only

*In Paint Shop Pro or Studio, choose File, Send to email the open image. This opens your email client with the picture set up as an attachment.*

Use image slicing to save an image into parts. This speeds up viewing of your site because optimized images take less time to download and parts used repeatedly are only saved once. Since many visitors lose patience if a site takes too long to download, this is vital. Slicing divides an image into editable "cells".

1 Choose File, Export, Image Slicer

2 Click a cell tool. (If you select Grid, also specify the no. of rows and columns)

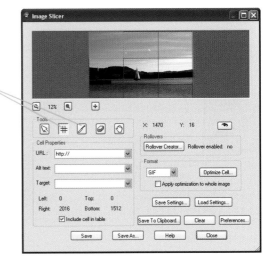

*In the Target field, you can choose from these options. With **_blank** the linked page opens in a new window. With **_parent** the linked page opens in the parent window. With **_self** the linked page opens in the same window and with **_top** it opens in the full browser window.*

3 If you chose Slicer in Step 2, click and drag over the Preview window to create horizontal and vertical lines. If you selected Grid instead (as here), just click in the Preview window

*You can create cells within cells, if you want. Just select a tool, click within one cell then define some more.*

4 Select the Arrow tool (the left-most tool in the dialog). Click a cell in the Preview window then edit it by completing the Properties section of the dialog. Also, select a format

5 Click Optimize Cell to launch the relevant file format dialog (see page 151) and complete this. Repeat 4–5 for each cell

6 You need to insert the slice settings into the image's HTML code. Click the Save to Clipboard button then complete the dialog. Open the HTML file and paste in the code at the right location

# Image mapping Paint Shop Pro 9 only

Use image mapping to create areas (hot spots) which are linked to Internet addresses (URLs). The hot spots are actually cells and can be circles, rectangles or irregular. When the site visitor moves his/her mouse pointer over a cell, it changes to a hand – this indicates that clicking it will jump to another Web page.

*To create a polygon, click to create a start point. Click elsewhere to create a line. Continue like this till you're thru – when the polygon is complete, right-click the image.*

1 Choose File, Export, Image Mapper

2 Click the Polygon, Rectangle or Circle tool, then click in the image preview

*Click Save Settings to save your area details for reuse in this or other images.*

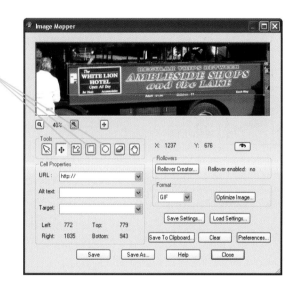

3 Drag out a map shape – here, a rectangle

*Set the appropriate option In the Target field (see the facing page).*

4 Select the Arrow tool (the left-most tool in the dialog). Click a map area in the Preview window then edit it by completing the Properties section of the dialog. Also, select a format

5 Click Optimize Image and complete the dialog box that launches by activating each tab and selecting the relevant options

6 You need to insert the map settings into the image's HTML code. Click the Save to Clipboard button then complete the two dialogs. Open the HTML file and paste in the code at the right location

# Photo Sharing

Paint Shop Pro and Studio support photo sharing. This means you can upload your images to online services and store them there. In this way, other people you invite can view and print them. Even better, there is no charge for the sharing service (though the companies listed below do charge for additional services such as photo printing).

At the time of writing, Studio supports the following online sharing services:

- PhotoBox (www.photobox.co.uk)

- Shutterfly (www.shutterfly.com)

Paint Shop Pro 9 also supports:

- Ofoto (www.ofoto.com/Welcome.isp)

*Online sharing services score in speed and ease of use. Sure, you could copy images to CD or DVD and pay to mail them out but they might get lost – even if they don't, they'll take a while to arrive. You could email them but here you come up against strict size limitations for attachments – if you make your favorite photo small enough to email, its quality will likely degrade unacceptably. Sharing your images online is a great alternative with no drawbacks.*

## Selecting an online service

1 Choose File, Preferences, General Program Preferences

2 Select the PhotoSharing tab

4 Select a service

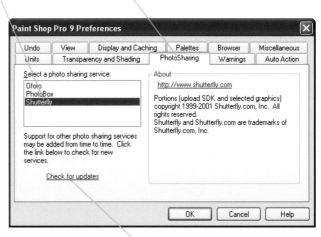

3 Optionally, ensure your Internet connection is live then click this to verify if Jasc has enabled any further sharing services

## Opening an account

1 Select File, Export, PhotoSharing

2 Select Create New Account

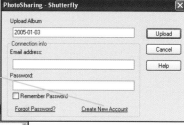

3 Complete the registration then click Join now

## Uploading

1 In the Paint Shop Pro or Studio Browser, right-click the photograph(s) you want to upload and select PhotoSharing

2 Complete the dialog (as above) but this time enter your email address and password. Click Upload and then Yes

## Sharing

1 On Shutterfly's website, select the Share online tab then follow the instructions

# Rollovers Paint Shop Pro 9 only

You can also export "rollovers". Rollovers are images or image sections that change into something else when activated by passing the mouse over them, and are often used on the Internet, particularly in website navigation bars.

The use of rollovers can make websites look much more graphically effective, and more professional.

## Creating rollovers

1 In the Image Slicer or Image Mapper dialogs (see pages 152 and 153), click the Arrow tool then select the cell or map area you want to convert to a rollover

2 Hit the Rollover Creator button

3 Select an initiating mouse action

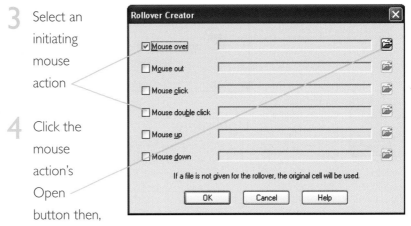

4 Click the mouse action's Open button then, in the Select Rollover dialog, select the image you want to use for the rollover

5 Repeat Steps 3–4 for each action that you want to associate with the rollover

6 Click OK

# Layers, masks and color corrections

## Chapter Eight

In this chapter, you'll enhance your use of images by working with layers and masks, advanced techniques that let you achieve unique effects. You'll also use Art Media layers for realistic painting effects and then create workspaces (so you can have different configurations of Paint Shop Pro for each job you do). You'll learn how to frame and border images and crop photographs to get rid of parts of images you don't want. You'll go on to work with histograms in order to readjust color values, and carry out other color corrections.

Finally, you'll print out your work, singly and with multiple images on the page.

## Covers

# Layers

*You can paint (or apply effects to) specific layers. When you do this, unaffected areas in underlying layers remain visible until you merge the layers.*

Layers are separate, transparent levels which add a new dimension to image editing, though they're not necessary for simple tasks. Memory permitting, you can have as many as 500 layers. Types of layer include:

## Raster

These host pixel-related data but can only be created in grayscale images or images with at least 16 million colors.

## Vector

These carry vector objects (e.g. shapes and text) and can be added to any image. Vector layers display icons representing each object.

## Adjustment

These contain color correction data but can only be created in grayscale images or images with at least 16 million colors.

*For obvious reasons, mask and adjustment layers can't be the bottom layer.*

## Mask

These show or hide underlying layers – see pages 169–174.

## Art Media

These are automatically created when you use any of the Art Media tools – see pages 167–168.

*In Studio, you can only create raster and vector layers.*

1    The Layers palette is where you work with layers. To launch or hide it, press F8

2    The toolbar – you can access most layer commands here

3    A vector object

4    Background layer – each new image has one. To promote it into a normal layer, right-click it in the palette. In the menu, select Promote To Layer

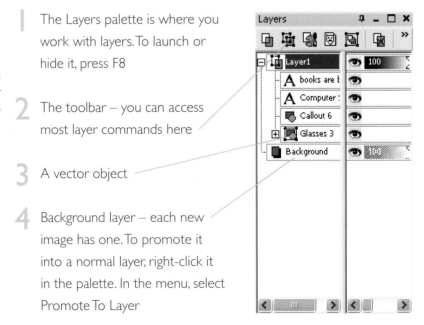

# Adding new layers

To create a new layer with default properties, hold down Shift as you click either of the layer creation buttons in the Layers palette toolbar.

Adjustment layers perform commands that are available on the Adjust menu; however, they don't change any pixels.

Use vector layers to create easily editable objects. They're really great for text.

1 Click one of the three icons on the left of the Layers palette toolbar, according to the type of layer you want to create

2 Or click a layer type in the Layer menu

3 If you chose New Adjustment Layer in Step 2, select a layer sub-type

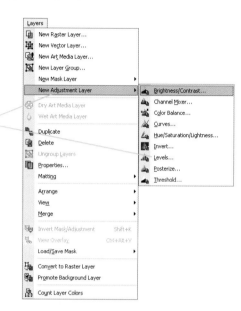

4 Name the layer

5 Work thru the tabs and their fields then click OK

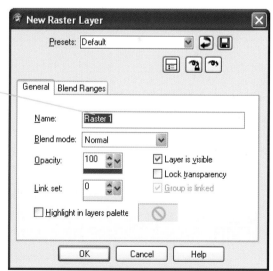

# Using the Layers palette

### Rearranging layers

1 Optionally, convert the Layers palette to a toolbar – you may find that this makes it easier to work with

*To delete a layer, right-click it in the Layers palette. Click Delete in the menu.*

2 Click a layer, then drag it up or down to a new location in the palette

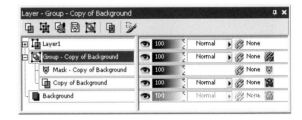

– this is called "promoting" it

### Merging layers

When you merge layers, you join all the component layers (or simply all visible layers) into one. As a result:

*Layer information is retained when you save your images to Paint Shop Pro's native format and also to Adobe Photoshop format.*

- they can no longer be edited independently

- all vector objects are rasterized

- all transparent areas are whitened

1 To merge all the layers within an image, pull down the Layers menu and select Merge All (Flatten)

2 Or, to merge only those layers currently visible within an image, pull down the Layers menu and select Merge Visible

### Duplicating layers

*Use duplicated layers to try out changes.*

1 Create a duplicate layer when you want to try out changes

2 Click this button in the toolbar:

## Hiding/showing layers or layer objects

In the Layers palette, click a layer's (or a vector object's) Visibility button to hide it – a red cross appears

*Current (visible) layers which hold no data are transparent.*

*Hold your mouse pointer over a layer's name to view a handy thumbnail.*

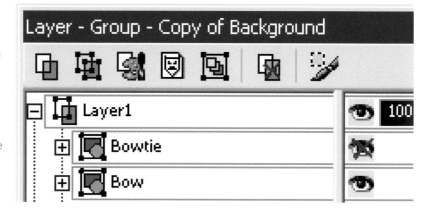

## Viewing/hiding all layers

To view or hide all layers, pull down the Layers menu and click View, All or View, None respectively

## Inverting layers

To make all invisible layers visible (or vice versa), pull down the Layers menu and click View, Invert

## Transporting selected layers to other images

In the Layers palette, drag the layer you want to copy onto the active image – the copied layer appears above the active one

*The destination image must be grayscale or 16-million-color.*

## Transporting all layers to other images

Hit Ctrl+B to launch the Browser

2 Drag the thumbnail for the image whose layers you want to copy onto the destination image

# Tips for using layers

1 Want to work on a photograph? You mostly won't need to use layers. For example, if you just want to crop out unwanted areas, why use layers? They'd just make the job unnecessarily complex

2 So why use layers? Let's say you wanted to make major changes to a photograph. Create a duplicate of the background layer then turn off the background's visibility. Now work away on the copy: if you don't like what you come up with, just delete the copy layer and there's no harm done

3 Want to add text? Don't do this directly onto the background. Instead, create a new vector layer and create the text here. Why? The text is much more easily editable

4 Use blend modes and ranges to customize how layers interact

5 Want to create a new vector illustration? Create each object on its own layer to aid editing

6 If vector objects on separate layers are logically related (e.g. someone riding a cycle) link them so if you move one onscreen, you move them all (you can also link groups)

7 Click in this field repeatedly till all layers you want to

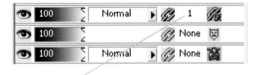

link have the same number. Linking only relates to the Move tool: it has no effect on the Layers palette stacking order

8 If you're working with multiple layers, turn off layer visibility selectively till you get the best result

# Layers in action

### Using blend modes

One great way to work with layers is to blend them. This simply involves controlling the way pixels on the layer to be blended interact with those on one or more underlying layers.

By default, the blend mode of all layers is "Normal". This means that pixels are blended with all underlying layers, not merely the one immediately below it. You can create some really unique effects by applying any of Paint Shop Pro or Studio's additional blend modes. The way each mode works can get quite technical – however, the best way to get to know them is to work through them and see the effects for yourself.

1 For the sake of demonstration, open one photograph

2 Open another. Press Ctrl+A to select it all then press Ctrl+C. These two photos are quite different, so they should give good results when blended

3　Back in the first photo, press Ctrl+L to insert the copy of the second as a new layer

4　This is what you'll see:

5　The first photo is the Background layer. The second is on Raster 1 – this is the layer we'll be blending

6　In the Layers palette, click in the Blend Mode field and make a choice in the list

*You are likely to get some cool effects by dragging the Opacity slider.*

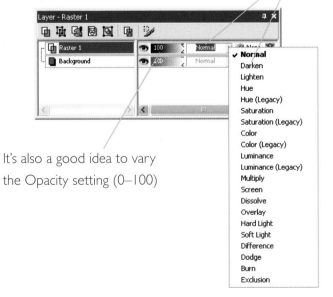

7　It's also a good idea to vary the Opacity setting (0–100)

8   The Lighten blend mode

9   The Difference blend mode

10   The Burn blend mode

## Using blend ranges

You can produce effects that are even more unique by limiting the pixels affected by blend modes.

1   Select a blend mode in the Layers palette then double-click the layer

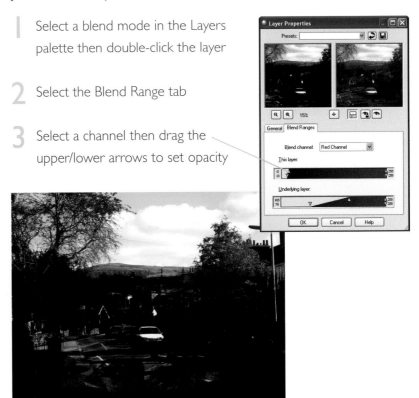

2   Select the Blend Range tab

3   Select a channel then drag the upper/lower arrows to set opacity

*The choice of channel determines how opacity is set.*

4   Here, varying the Red Channel opacity has made quite a difference to a Burn blend

# Art Media layers **Paint Shop Pro 9 only**

Paint Shop Pro now has a special class of layer called Art Media. As we've seen in Chapter 1, when you create a new image you have the option of creating it with an Art Media background (in other words, it automatically has an Art Media layer). We'll look at this process in more detail now:

1   Press the Ctrl+N keys

2   Select Art Media Background

3   To increase the realism, apply an artistic texture. Click here and choose one from the list

4   Optionally, select a fill color

5   Click OK

6   This is what you get. Instead of a layer called Background, the base layer is Art Media

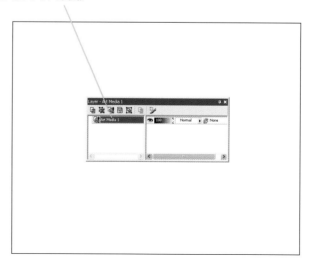

7   Alternatively, you can insert an Art Media layer into an existing image (particularly useful if you want to apply painting effects to photographs). In your image, select Layers, New Art Media Layer

8   Select an Art Media tool and begin painting:

*Painting with the Art Media tools directly onto a raster layer automatically creates an Art Media layer.*

9   Experiment with differing blend moles. This is Exclusion:

# Masks Paint Shop Pro 9 only

*Because masks are bitmaps, all bitmap tools work with them. Also, in those tools which have bitmap and vector modes, only the bitmap component is operative on masks.*

Masks are specialized, 256-color grayscale layers that are overlaid over other layers. They contain "holes"; you perform editing operations on the areas displayed through the gaps. The holes can be created via selection areas, other images or channels. Alternatively, the mask can be as large as the underlying layer. Use masks to create fades between layers or to create special effects that would otherwise be difficult or impossible to achieve.

To an extent, then, masks can be regarded as stencils. However, they also act as advanced selection areas. For example, you can control the extent to which a mask operates by defining the grayscale content:

- painting with black hides underlying layers

- painting with white makes underlying layers visible

- painting with any intervening shade of gray allows a portion of the effect you generate to take effect

*You can apply any filter, deformation or effect which can be used with grayscale images.*

Here, a separate image has been applied as a mask and a fill has been applied to it:

# Layer masks

## Masking an entire layer

1 Select the layer you want to mask

*If you try to mask the Background layer, you'll be asked whether you want Paint Shop Pro to promote it first. Accept the suggestion.*

2 Select Layer, New Mask Layer

3 In the sub-menu, select Show All to view all the underlying pixels or Hide All for the reverse

4 If you selected Show All, initially the only evidence that a new mask has been added is a new entry in the Layers palette

*When you create any kind of mask, the mask layer and the active layer are automatically grouped. As a result, the mask only applies to this layer (but you can drag it anywhere else in the Layers palette).*

*You can edit the mask later to mask selective areas.*

# Selection masks

Selection masks are masks which contain a hole (the hole being supplied by the selection area). By default, any changes you make apply to the hole, not the surrounding area.

### Creating a selection mask

1 Define the appropriate selection area

2 Pull down the Layer menu and select New Mask Layer. In the sub-menu, select Hide Selection or Show Selection

3 This is Hide Selection. To make the mask itself visible (this applies to all mask types), press Ctrl+Alt+V:

*Press Ctrl+D to remove the original selection.*

# Image masks

### Creating masks from images

If you've split
an image into
RGB, HSL (Hue,
Saturation and
Lightness) or
CMYK channels (Image, Split
Channels...), you can select one in
Step 4 to apply it as a layer.

1 Open the image
you want to use
as a mask and
then the image
you want to
insert it into

Created a cool
mask? Save it to
disk for reuse.
Choose Layers,
Load/Save Mask,
Save Mask To Disk.

2 In the destination image, select the layer you want to mask then
select Layers, New Mask Layer, From Image

3 Select the mask image then OK

4 The result with the mask made
visible (Ctrl+Alt+V):

### Loading masks from disk

1  You can also load masks from disk. This is especially useful as Paint Shop Pro comes with numerous masks ready for use

2  Select Layers, Load/Save Mask, Load Mask From Disk

3  Select a mask then customize how it functions (Create mask from), how it aligns with the layer (Orientation) and how much of it is visible (Options)

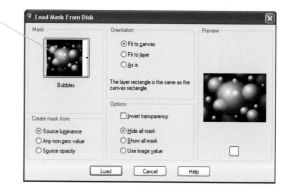

4  After applying the Bubbles mask that ships with Paint Shop Pro – the mask is the checkered area

# Editing masks

*A quick way to dramatically change a mask is to invert its transparency by hitting Shift+K.*

## Amending a mask

1  Select the mask layer in the Layers palette

2  In previous versions of Paint Shop Pro, it was necessary to enter a special state known as Edit Mode in order to edit masks. Now, however, as soon as a mask is created, it's ready to edit

*When you select a mask layer, the Materials palette shows grayscales.*

3  Paint with any of the painting tools (e.g. the Brush tool) to amend the mask area. Painting with white will not affect the mask since white represents 0% opacity. Instead, use darker shades of white, gray or black to edit your mask

4  Try this for a quick effect. Set the Foreground/Stroke to the Black-white gradient then use the Flood Fill tool to fill the mask with it. The black areas hide the mask, the white areas display it

5  Edit the mask layer's opacity or visibility

*You can add any filter, deformation or effect to masks (but the process may take longer than usual).*

6  A photograph with the Cubes mask applied and made visible:

# Histogram adjustments Paint Shop Pro 9 only

You can make various adjustments to image color distribution via the Histogram window.

*Move your mouse pointer over any point in the Histogram window to display (on the right) the percentage of pixels that are below or above it or in the same range. (You can also drag out a selection in the window and get the same information.)*

1 Open the image you want to adjust

2 Press F7

3 The three RGB components (Red, Green and Blue) display horizontally. The vertical axis against which these are plotted represents each component's share of colors in pixels. The far left of the horizontal axis represents black, the far right white. Spikes indicate a concentration of a particular value – in other words, lots of pixels

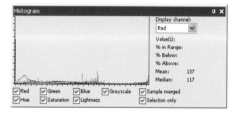

4 It doesn't particularly apply here, but if Grayscale is checked and the spread is largely at the left, the image is too dark. The opposite also applies

5 If Sample merged is checked, the Histogram window graphs all layers in the image

6 The wide horizontal spread indicates the image could do with some adjustment – see over

7 The image from page 175 after One Step Photo Fix has been applied

8 And the changed Histogram window. Notice that the spread is less flat – the result is a better photograph

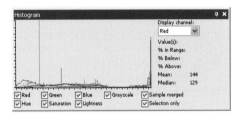

*Equalize rearranges image pixels so that those around the midpoint of the relevant histogram are pushed nearer the high and low brightness levels. The result is normally an averaging of image brightness. Stretch has somewhat the opposite effect. In images where black and white are not included in the histogram, it ensures the colors do span the full spectrum.*

## Applying Equalize or Stretch

You can carry out two principal histogram-based operations on images: Equalize and Stretch.

1 Press Shift+E to Equalize or Shift+T to Stretch

2 After applying Equalize

# Framing

When you've got your image looking really good, you can frame it.

1 Choose Image, Picture Frame

2 Select a frame

3 Click a position then OK

*To border an image, pull down the Image menu and select Add Borders. Specify a color and which sides you want bordered.*

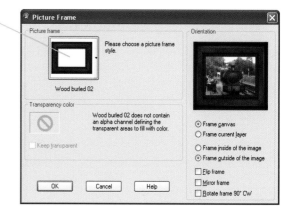

4 Why not frame images you've applied special effects to?

# Cropping

Cropping means telling Paint Shop Pro or Studio what part of an image you want to keep and discarding the rest. Photographs often need to be cropped for printing; also, cropping is a great way to enhance photos so they only show what you want to see.

## Method I

1 Define a selection area with the appropriate selection tool

*The disadvantage of using the selection tool method is that you can't resize the selection area.*

2 You can use the Tool Options palette to customize the selection

3 Press Shift+R to discard the image area outside the selection

*The Crop tool comes with useful presets in the Tool Options palette. For example, if you want to print your photographs on 10cm x 15cm glossy paper, you can save a lot of time by applying the preset for it.*

*To turn off shading, select File, Preferences, General Program Preferences. Select the Transparency and Shading tab then uncheck Enable crop shade area.*

## Method 2

1 If you're working on a background layer, promote it

2 Press R to launch the Crop tool

3 Drag out a crop box

4 Notice that the area outside the crop box is now shaded, so you can see the difference more easily

5 To move (but not resize) the crop rectangle, click inside it and drag to a new location. To resize the rectangle, drag one of the sides or corners in or out

6 Double-click inside the crop box – the image is cropped:

# Workspaces Paint Shop Pro 9 only

You can save details of your "workspace" so you can have different configurations for different purposes. This means all your palettes, toolbars, zoom settings, grid/ruler settings and open images.

*When you create a workspace, you're prompted to save any unnamed images,* and any previously named but amended files are saved automatically.

## Saving workspaces

1 Get Paint Shop Pro looking the way you want it then hit Shift+Alt+S

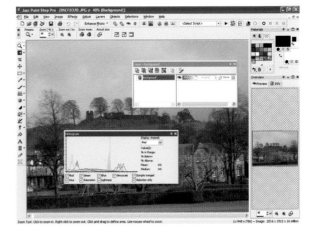

*The workspace only stores details of where the relevant files are located, not the files themselves.*

2 Name the workspace in the dialog then hit Save

## Loading workspaces

1 Hit Shift+Alt+L then double-click a workspace in the dialog

2 The same screen components launch but, for some reason, image windows aren't maximized

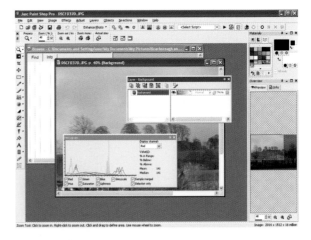

# Printing single images

## Printing the active image

1 Hit Ctrl+P

2 Select a printer then adjust its settings

*Select a print orientation in the Orientation section then (if you haven't chosen a template) allocate a size/position option.*

3 Type in the no. of copies

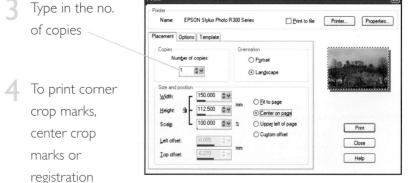

4 To print corner crop marks, center crop marks or registration marks, select the Options tab and check the relevant option(s). Crop and registration marks help commercial printers ensure print and color accuracy and mainly apply to PostScript output. If you're printing to a desktop printer, you won't require any of these features

*To print to a file (e.g. for submission to a commercial printer), check Print to file and complete the dialog that launches.*

5 To print the filename – or any title entered in the Current Image Information dialog – check Image Name under the Options tab

6 Under Options, check Grayscale to print out in gray shades

*Want to print out your image in negative? Just select the Options tab and check Negative.*

7 Select the Template tab to print a template (see also overleaf) with your image or to have your image fill a template. Check Print to template then choose one in the dialog

8 Click Print to begin printing

# Printing multiple images

Paint Shop Pro has a neat way to print more than one image on the same page: the Print Layout Window.

1 Choose File, Print Layout

2 All currently open images are shown as thumbnails (to open more, choose File, Open Image and complete the dialog)

*If the layout you're printing is one you use frequently, save it as a template so you can reuse it. Choose File, Save Template. Complete the dialog – check Save with images if you want the images currently displayed to open when you reopen the template.*

3 Drag the thumbnails you want to print onto the page – use the mouse to move or resize them

*You need to ensure you print images with the correct resolution. Use the following guide. For 300 dpi (dots per inch) printing, use an image resolution of 72–120. For 600 dpi printing, use 125–170.*

4 To insert a text caption, click **A** in the toolbar. Click where you want to insert the text then complete the dialog

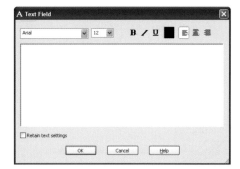

5 Optionally, click an image and apply any relevant menu commands (e.g. to view information about the image, select Image information in the Edit menu)

6 Choose File, Print to begin printing

# Scripts **Paint Shop Pro 9 only**

In this chapter, you'll learn about a great productivity tool. You'll record just about any Paint Shop Pro procedure or series of procedures and save them as a script. You can then apply them at any point, just by selecting and running the script. You can also edit scripts and even apply the same script to multiple images in one go.

## Covers

**Chapter Nine**

# Generating and playing scripts

In Paint Shop Pro 9 you can automate lengthy tasks. We all have procedures we do fairly often and these are often complex. The good news is that you can record these as "scripts" and play them back. The bad news is that there are certain restrictions:

*Those skilled at programming can find out more about Python (Paint Shop Pro's scripting engine) at http://www.python.org/.*

- customizations of the user interface or operations inside Print Layout can't be scripted

- operations involving the Materials or Mixer palette can't be recorded on-the-fly (but they can be written with a text editor, which requires some programming expertise)

- some plug-ins may not be scriptable

## Recording a script

1   Make a written note of the actions you want to record

2   Launch the Script toolbar (View, Toolbars, Script)

3   Click here

4   Carry out the actions you listed

*Presets are scripts. So, basically, are print layouts.*

5   Click here

*You can have up to 9 BoundScripts. These are special scripts which can be dragged onto toolbars and menus and can be assigned keyboard shortcuts.*

**6** Go to the right folder then name the script

**7** Click Save

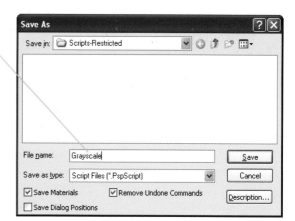

*Because of the connection with Python, scripts can be "restricted" or "trusted". Most of the difference has to do with security; in practical terms, the main point is that some commands (like File, Save As) can't be run from protected scripts.*

## Running a script

**1** Select a script

**2** Click here

**3** Alternatively, if the script isn't visible in the list, click this button:

**4** In the dialog, find the script, select it then hit Open to run it

# Editing scripts

*Can't find the script? Choose File, Script, Edit and locate then open it with the dialog that launches.*

Paint Shop Pro has a built-in script editor which should enable just about anyone to edit some aspects of scripts. (Programming gurus can also edit scripts in text editors like Notepad.)

## Using the built-in editor

Select a script in the Script toolbar then click this button:

*If the script was created with a text editor, this dialog doesn't appear. Instead, the script opens in your default text editor.*

2 Uncheck a script component to disable it

3 Select a component (some can't be edited) then hit Edit. Modify the command's settings in the originating dialog etc.

## Advanced editing

*You can apply scripts to multiple files at once. Hit File, Batch, Process. Go to the folder which hosts the files you want to process then flag them. Select a Save Mode. Check Use Script, choose a script then customize the output format/ folder. Hit Start to begin the batch process.*

1 Want to edit a script at source? Hit Text Editor in the Script Editor dialog box

2 Edit it in the usual manner

# Index